Journey to The People

ALSO BY ANN NOLAN CLARK

Along Sandy Trails

In My Mother's House

Little Navajo Bluebird

Magic Money

Secret of the Andes

Looking-for-Something

Blue Canyon Horse

Santiago

The Desert People

Tia Maria's Garden

Bear Cub

ANN NOLAN CLARK

Journey

to

The People

WITH AN INTRODUCTION

BY ANNIS DUFF

THE VIKING PRESS

NEW YORK

Library of Congress catalog card number: 75-88623. Printed in U.S.A. by The Book Press.

372   1. Teaching
2. American Indian children

To Annis Duff,

my editor

and my friend

Contents

Introduction

The publication in 1941 of Ann Nolan Clark's *In My Mother's House* was a literary landmark in two respects: this was the first children's book written about Indian children of the American Southwest from the viewpoint of the Indian children themselves; and it was the first of numbers of distinguished children's books to come out of the author's long, rich, and varied experience as a teacher among the Indian peoples of North, Central, and South America.

Ann Clark had not wanted to be a teacher in the first place. She wanted to write. But writing provides too precarious a livelihood for a young woman who must be independent, and teaching seemed the safe and logical profession for her to follow. If she could have foreseen what complicated and arduous situations her own abilities would lead her into she might scarcely have thought of it as "safe." But fortunately she had gifts of character, intelligence, sympathy, imagination, and stamina that enabled her to develop a career of notable service and value.

Her first position was in a German community in New Mexico, where room—hers was in a loft!—and board were part of a none-too-generous salary. Here her sole identity was simply as "Teacher," and she disliked the name. But she was a real teacher, and she began to find this out through her adjustability to a new way of living and to the different kinds of people she was associated with.

After her second teaching experience—this was in a small ungraded school in a mining town in New Mexico—she married, and in 1920 her son was born. Several years later she returned to work, as she says, "browsing in and out of Indian schools." On two different occasions she was a substitute teacher at the Pueblo of Zuñi, living at the Blackrock Boarding School forty-odd miles from Gallup, and she taught for several months at Tesuque, near Santa Fé.

Then, she says, an official of the Branch of Education of the United States Bureau of Indian Affairs "talked me into taking the examinations and becoming a permanent employee in the Indian Service." Her first assignment was at the Santa Fé Boarding School, where she taught for several years. During this time John Collier became Commissioner of Indian Affairs, and he held an all-Pueblo council at Santo Domingo in central New Mexico. He asked the representatives of each Pueblo reservation what they wanted, and the Tesuque Pueblo wanted Ann Clark as a teacher there.

The Santa Fé superintendent did not want her to go, thinking it would be a mistake professionally for her to transfer from a large boarding school to a one-teacher school. But she thought differently, and she went. This was where she knew she belonged. For she "saw something awful happening to Indian children and was beginning to see why." Here were children with ancient culture patterns bred into their bones, expected to assimilate ways of living, thinking, and learning that were totally unrelated to anything they had ever known, and with little meaning to them *as Indians.* An attempt was being made, with however good intentions, to turn them into "average" Americans, their own particular needs and natures having too little consideration in the general scheme of Indian education. Ann Clark dedicated herself to doing whatever she was able in helping to correct this situation.

It was during her four years of work in Tesuque that "one thing happened to make a great difference." This was the writing of the home geography that later became, as she tells in Chapter Four, *In My Mother's House.* Someone—she is not sure who—took the calico-covered book to Washington, D.C., and it eventually found its way to The Viking Press in New York and became Ann Nolan Clark's first published book.

Now came ever-widening opportunities and responsibilities. Willard Beatty, Chief, Branch of Education, Bureau of Indian Affairs, believed firmly that Indian children have the right to identify with children in books. But there had been no books about children sufficiently like themselves in ways of living to provide any basis for identification. *In My Mother's House* unquestionably made "a great difference" in this condition of things. It has the texture and cadence of Tewa Indian speech, and a deep feeling for the world the Indian child knows.

Mr. Beatty wanted to have books written, in both English and Indian languages, and he wisely saw that Ann Clark was the ideal person to write the English versions. She said she would try, and with a group of anthropologists working with Indian translators to provide the various Indian language versions, she produced something like twenty books. During the preparation of these she lived among the Pueblo, Navajo, Zuñi, and Dakota Sioux peoples.

Mr. Beatty's next enterprise was a monthly magazine for all intermediate-grade Indian children of the United States, and he asked Ann Clark if she would edit it. Again she said she would try, and again she justified his confidence in her by getting six issues ready in advance of first publication.

While she was at work on this formidable undertaking, World War II began, and she was sent as a member of an Indian Service team to establish schools in a Japanese re-habilitation center. A short time later all Indian Service publishing came to an end because of the war, and Mr. Beatty asked Ann Clark to go as a supervisor to the Papago and the Pima of southern Arizona. While she was there her son was killed in a gallant and successful effort to ensure the safety of the men in a flying mission over the Pacific. His mother was urged to go home to Santa Fé, where he had grown up, and she went as a supervisor to the Northern Pueblos.

Then a change in her work came in a most unexpected way. She happened to be on a school visit in Taos when a three-way telephone call—between Washington, Guatemala and New Mexico—brought her an invitation to go to Cen-tral and South America, in the service of the Institute of Inter-American Affairs, as a writer of simple reading mate-rials for use in teaching there. She accepted, but when she arrived she found that the procedures for teaching reading were so different from those she had used that she had to help train the teachers as well as write the books. She decided, too, that it would be better if they, not she, wrote the books, and she trained them to do this.

Her own account of the varying degrees of success in her work in Latin America is characteristically laconic:

> Guatemala—very successful.
> Honduras—did nothing. They had a revolution.
> Panama—so-so results.
> Costa Rica—good training program. No books.
> Ecuador—very good.
> Peru—good.

She had asked for only one year's leave of absence from the Indian Service to do her work for the Institute of Inter-American Affairs, but she stayed for eight years in the various southern countries. During that time she was loaned to U.N.E.S.C.O. to go to Paris to participate in a conference on minority groups and to go to Brazil to work with newly literate people.

While she was away from the United States Willard Beatty started the Five-year Special Navajo Program (which lasted for about fifteen years) and he repeatedly reminded her that her year's leave of absence had expired. He wanted her to write materials for his program. At last she consented to come home, but only on condition that she could be free from time to time to go back to finish the work she had begun in Latin America.

When Mrs. Hildegard Thompson succeeded Willard Beatty as Chief of the Branch of Education of the Bureau of Indian Affairs, she asked Ann Clark to write the books that were needed for Adult Indian Education. Mrs. Clark undertook this new assignment with typical thoroughness, and once again exceeded the specified requirements of the job. She trained teachers to write their own materials, and probably a hundred books were produced, manuals for the many crafts and skills that were taught to equip Indians for useful, productive work away from their reservations.

Then, in 1962, after a serious injury that kept her in the hospital for many months, this indomitable lady realized that the time had come for her to be relieved of the strenuous demands of her professional life. On her retirement the United States Department of the Interior, in recognition of her splendid accomplishments in the field of Indian education, conferred on her the Distinguished Service Award.

This was not the first or the only reward to come to Ann Nolan Clark. It must be remembered that through the years of what seems to the beholder an almost superhuman professional effort, she continued to write for the general public of children and young people. Her first book was a prize winner in the New York *Herald Tribune* Children's Spring Book Festival; the Newbery Medal of the American Library Association was awarded to *Secret of the Andes* as "the most distinguished book for children" published in 1952; and in 1963 the Regina Medal of the Catholic Library Association was bestowed on her for "continued distinguished contribution to literature for children." But while medals and honors are "happy happenings," she finds her real reward in the interest, confidence, and affection of her continually growing body of young readers.

Once a group of eight or ten Haitians—"very black, very

smart, very wonderful, and very dear people"—participated in one of Ann Clark's teacher-training courses. Many years afterward she received an Easter card from them with this simple message, "Mother, you still haunt us." This is easy to understand. Nobody who has ever known her, as a person, as a teacher, or through her books, could ever forget her. Quiet, unassuming, grave and merry by turns, possessed of boundless compassion and a fine sense of humor, she is a rare and shining human being. How fortunate it is that writer and teacher grew together in one person, to bring enlightenment, beauty, and joy into so many lives!

ANNIS DUFF

Baltimore
May 1969

Journey to The People

ONE

Cultural Differences

I was once asked to talk to a group of librarians about the culturally disadvantaged children who stand before the books on their bookshelves and walk through their libraries. I thought about this topic for a long time and decided, at last, that I could not talk about culturally disadvantaged children because I do not think of them in this way. I have spent my adult life working in one field or another with children of different minority groups, but never have I thought of them as disadvantaged culturally. Rather, I think of them as children whose culture patterns differ from my own. In my thinking the word "culture" does not mean the educational standard of *my* group but rather the behavior pattern of *any* group.

I told my listeners that if they would permit me to use my meaning of the word "culture," then I could talk happily and, perhaps, to some good, about some of the cultural differences that exist between our group pattern and the group patterns of many of our Southwestern children. I am not going to discuss whether we should or should not try to change group characteristics, but to point out that there are differences which have existed since group patterns were formed. These differences are lessening slowly as the larger group grinds against and wears away the pattern designs of the smaller groups. New concepts are developed by individuals within the groups, but also, in many cases, new ideas have been merely superimposed upon age-old characteristics, causing uncertainty and confusion.

Child characteristics are similar for all children. These we can cope with because we understand them. But racial characteristics differ, and these differences we must recognize and accept; not necessarily understand or approve them, but meet them with an awareness of their importance and with a tolerance born of the knowledge that our culture also differs from other group norms. A child can carry a lasting scar without knowing what caused the wound. Many of our Southwestern children stand in two worlds of conflicting concepts. Our job is to know this and to help each child build his bridges with confidence, security, and courage.

My concern is for Indian children, because racial differences are greater than those of nationalities. Generally, differences in traditions and customs can be met to mutual satisfaction with mutual generosity and humor. Differences of concepts, however, are more difficult to understand and more difficult to accept. I believe there are four Indian *group* concepts that differ greatly from concepts in our group pattern. These are the Indian feeling about land, about work, about time, and about the spiritual life.

There is a feeling about land. White American culture thinks of land as a property having a salable value. It can be owned by an individual or, under prescribed conditions, by a group. It can be taken or lost by conquest; forfeited or given by treaty; given by grant; received by inheritance; rented; bought and sold. Land is considered as an object having value that can be owned and exchanged.

This concept was, and to some extent still is, strange to the Indian. Land, to him, is the place where his ancestors lived, hunted, made their camp circles, and lighted their cooking fires. It was not owned by an individual or a group as an object having a salable value. It was a life factor that was used as the sun and the water and the air were used. It became part of the life way of the people who used it. The Indian felt a relationship with his land; a brotherhood existed between man and the earth he walked upon. He petitioned it to give food to his people in the same way that he petitioned the sun to give warmth and the clouds to give rain.

Land was not exchanged. It was never fought over for ownership, only for the use of the game trails. As the Indian petitioned his land, he also adjusted his life to fit into his environment. He did not try to change it to meet his fancy or his needs. He never moved mountains or changed the river courses. When an alien racial group came in and claimed his land it was as incomprehensible to him as if it had claimed the sun or the wind or the rain.

He could not understand how land could be divided into pieces and a designated portion given to him as his reservation. He could not understand how land that was a life factor could be considered as an object tossed from hand to hand as a ball was tossed on the ball court of his ancients. Neither could he understand that straight lines drawn on a piece of paper and meeting to form squares and rectangles could mean land divided by boundary lines. The boundary of a land site was, to him, a natural line determined by a distant peak, a cloud-crowned mesa, a dry sand wash, or a river bed. An old Shoshoni Bannock Indian once told me that "Whiteman's" insistence upon land's having straight lines meeting to make corners had caused the never-to-be-forgotten trouble between his people and mine. "Land," he said, "must have natural lines as the Giver-of-Life made them when he made the land, never lines making corners and made by man on a piece of paper." When I left him he was still shaking his head and mumbling, "Land has no corners."

This difference in land concept seemingly causes little trouble today. Our concept seemingly has been accepted, but the wound remains—not the scar, the wound—and the wound has not completely healed.

As the Indian felt that the land was to be used, so did he feel that the things the land gave him were for his use. He felt that the fruits and nuts of the trees, the berries on the bushes, the game animals of mountain and valley, and the fish in the lakes and the rivers were for the users. All Southwestern Indian groups still petition the land to be bountiful and lavish with its gifts so that life can be sustained.

Teen-age Navajo children who had not been to school before were taken to a large government Indian boarding school in California for training. For a month or so of each new school year there never seemed to be a day when some child did not disappear for a little while and return in triumph with his blanket full of oranges from someone's citrus grove and his hat full of goldfish from someone's garden pool. To an Indian, stealing is very wrong, but to steal is to take an object that is someone's property. Who could steal the warmth of a sunray or the wetness of a raindrop or a gift from the land? Who could take these things and be called thief?

What we do to children—not knowing! But we must learn to know and we must learn to care.

In northern New Mexico, to this day, the piñon nuts on the stunted pine trees belong to the people who decide to pick them. A landowner who is annoyed at seeing large families of people he does not know picnicking in his driveway, getting water from his sprinkling system, walking through his patio, and picking his piñons learns to go away for the weekends of the piñon-picking season. Upon his return he may find, but not always, a small paper bag filled with piñons at his door. Not by way of thank you—never thank you—but a joyful sharing of the generosity of the land. After a while he may even like the idea that the patch of stunted piñons on the sandy hillside that he thinks he owns can be so royal in its giving at the harvest of its year.

There is a feeling about work. In the traditional Indian culture an Indian did not work for money. He did not work in exchange for things. He did not work for pay of any kind. An Indian worked because the work in itself was important to his own, his family's, or his community's welfare. If he did not consider the work necessary, he did not do it.

Trade articles were bartered for, but these were articles of ornament or for ceremonial use. They were not the necessary things of every day, as for example moccasins or mantas. When moccasins were needed, they were made. Someone killed a deer, someone tanned its hide, someone cut and sewed the moccasins. When a manta was needed, it also was made. Someone planted the cotton, someone spun the thread, then someone wove the garment. All of this was produced by family or clan members. A house was built by relatives and clan members. The group worked together at tasks that were for the common good. There were no services for hire. Work for the family was done by the family.

Working by the hour, day, week, or month was unknown. Much of the work was seasonal and therefore had to be undertaken at certain seasons and its completion time was determined by seasonal factors. An individual worked steadily at what needed to be accomplished until the finished product resulted. Then no one worked until it again became necessary. Work well done was its reward, not the quantity nor the quickness, nor the time taken to complete it. Work was a necessity, never a "pass-time."

An Indian works to live. In the middle-class white world we live to work. There is a wide difference between these two concepts. If we are aware that the difference exists and what the different group viewpoints are, we may be less prone to describe an Indian's work habits as those of a lazy, incompetent person. The Indian is not lazy. He has infinite patience and infinite endurance and infinite steadfastness in doing work that seems to him important enough to be done.

There is a feeling about time. In the Indian's thinking all his time concepts conflict with ours. White children are kept as infants for a very much longer period than is granted to the Indian child. From the moment of birth an Indian

23

child enters an adult world. He has his place as a family member. He is neither coddled nor petted but is respected and trusted as the other members of his family are respected and trusted. An Indian does not believe that "a child should be seen and not heard." An Indian child is listened to, his opinions and wants are given careful consideration. Age is venerated. This veneration is not compelled but given freely out of respect and love. In Indian culture punishment is the disapproval of one's peers. In the old days a child was neither scolded nor struck. He was reasoned with, and if reasoning failed there was disapproval, silent, but so keen its sting was more hurtful than a slap. The Indian child matures early. He is ready for man's estate long before he has completed the white standard of education.

An Indian looks backward to the ways of his ancients. It is difficult for him to change. It is difficult for him to apply old norms in new ways. He finds sequence almost incomprehensible. He is very creative, but in a rigidly determined pattern. He is naturally slow and deliberate and associates "hurry" with slipshod accomplishments. Keeping to a schedule broken into hours and half hours is an agony for both himself and the schedule maker. Sun time and moon time are his natural clocks. Once when I asked an Indian mother why her small Ygnacio was so slow in learning "how to tell time," she answered, "Oh, he knows what you want him to do, but he does not think it is good to break the day into little pieces."

There is a feeling about the spiritual life. The Southwestern Indian is a deeply reverent person. Before his ancient culture pattern was cut and parts of it discarded and new parts added in patches or appliqué, his whole life way fitted into and merged and blended with his environment and the physical and symbolic phenomena of his natural world. His entire life was spent in acts of petition and thanksgiving to Life Power. No task was undertaken without asking that its fulfillment be for the people's good; from the sunrise call, pleading that the new day be blessed, to the scattering of his thoughts at evening, his day was a continual prayer. When he built a house he asked a blessing of its essence before his family partook of its shelter. Before he planted his crops he asked the land to receive the seeds he gave it and to bless them into fruitage for his needs, and in reverence he walked barefoot over the newly turned earth so as not to bruise Earth Mother in her season of bearing. At harvest he gave communal ceremonies to thank the earth and the sun and the rain for the foods of the field. When he killed a deer he asked its spirit to bless its flesh against man's hunger of winter. When the group went on communal hunts or on pilgrimages for salt they asked the game animals or the salt pits to give generously of themselves that men, their brothers, have continuing life. They did this in ancient times and they still do this in the privacy of the mountains and the marshes that are left to them. In Indian culture there is a communion between the physical and the spiritual world that members of our culture group do not have—or have lost, if we ever had it. We must be aware that this oneness between an Indian child and his spirituality can be taken from him and nothing as completely satisfying be given him to fill the void. It is not for us to say what is good or bad or right or wrong. Our mission is to recognize that there are differ-

ences and to lead the child, who may be stumbling among
the terrifying boulders of differences in belief, to a quiet
and safe haven where awareness comes from the heart and
acceptance from the intellect, and tolerance is not a word to
say but a way of life.

> In the house of life I wander
> with beauty before and behind me,
> with beauty above and below me,
> with beauty within and around me,
> To old age traveling
> on the beautiful trail of life.

TWO

Traditions and Customs

In my many years of teaching children and in helping to train others to teach them, the realization has come to me again and again that different children have different traditions and customs from the larger group in which they find themselves and need much more than food, shelter, and clothing. Food, shelter, and clothing are basic needs, basic tangibles, but there are basic intangibles that also have importance.

There is need for awareness that each group of people has its own special traditions and customs. There is need that respectful recognition be given these special traditions and customs. There is need for acceptance of these differences. There is tragic need for loving communion between children and children, children and adults, adults and adults— between group and group.

Our white American culture has a tendency to set up its traditions and cultures as the norm, the principle of rightness which guides and regulates acceptable beliefs and acceptable behavior. Strange traditions and customs, especially those of other races, we tend to dismiss as peculiarities or superstitions. This feeling of our group makes impenetrable barriers to harmonious relationships with others. These barriers must come down, and each member of each group must do his part to bring them down.

Traditions are the inherited thought patterns of a people. They are beliefs that have been handed down from generation to generation until they have become a part of a people's blood and bone. If people have their beliefs taken from them and are given as replacement nothing that they can hold to, can live by, with peace of mind and serenity of heart, they become a people bewildered, confused, or defiant.

Customs are the inherited behavior pattern of a group. They, too, have been handed down through the generations. For a people to change its customs is not as shattering as to break with its traditions. But custom changing is a difficult and slow process because many customs have their beginning in tradition, even though through the years this fact may have been forgotten. Many customs should change not because one group demands it of another group but because situations, conditions, and problems change and new customs come into being to meet these changes. The people themselves must make the change.

When I say that difference of tradition and custom must be recognized and accepted, I do not say that there must be an understanding of the reasons that make the differences. I think there must be acceptance, whether or not it is reinforced by understanding.

Many times I have accepted a difference of belief or a manner of doing and only weeks, months, even years afterward have come to understand the reason. You cannot know how grateful I have been that I had not demanded an explanation but had accepted that which *was*. I was not born with this gift of acceptance but had to learn it painfully and often with hurt to others.

Memories crowd in upon me—fifty years of memories of working with peoples whose traditions and customs differed from those that were handed down to me. One memory is of my first learning that different traditions and customs must be recognized, respected, and accepted. This lesson was taught me at my first Indian day school, where I taught Indian children and lived as a part of an Indian community. The occasion was a dinner party I planned for five old Indian potters and their husbands.

These Indians were Tewa, gentle, laughing, loving people, yet unmovable when it came to changing ways that had been theirs for uncounted centuries. At the time I did not know what could have caused them to act as they did. Now I know it was a not-being-able-to-change. They could not bring themselves to do what we had agreed upon, as it was not a custom and was not in their tradition.

Tesuque is a Tewa village near Santa Fé, in northern New Mexico. Its name means "place-where-the-cottonwood-trees-grow-by-the-river." These people were living in this small village when the conquistadors came into this country. They are a slow, deliberate people, holding safe their children, their lands, their traditions, their customs.

The dinner party was to be a reward to these five Indian women who had gone back to their traditional way of making pottery. Their grandmothers had taught them this way as they themselves had been taught by their grandmothers; but in later years ancient techniques were not being used and were in danger of being forgotten. It took a bit of coaxing on my part to persuade them to bring out the "old-fashioned pots" from the dark corners of crowded storerooms and to fashion new ones like them, using the old techniques. They did it more to please my mother, who was living with me at that time, than because the old techniques had value in their eyes.

After they had made the pots, I asked them what I could do to show them how pleased I was with what they had done. They talked quietly in Tewa for a while, then told me softly, "Invite us to dinner and to bring our husbands." This surprised me, for we often had school parties for which the entire village came to the schoolhouse and feasted on corn, meat and chili, bread, and beans. This time, they said, they did not want an Indian feast, but a "white-people dinner" —"a dinner like white people have." A white-people dinner!

What would I give them? It was not Thanksgiving or Christmas or New Year's or Easter, when white people have special foods to fit the occasion. This was just an ordinary time of year. So I decided to give them that kind of dinner. I chose my menu from one of my mother's Sunday dinners of my childhood—roast beef, mashed potatoes and gravy, peas, a fruit salad, hot rolls and butter, apple pie.

They were delighted. That was what they wanted—no chili, no corn, no beans. A white-people dinner! We chose a day a week away and all through the week they came to ask, "You invited us? We are coming?"

At last the day arrived, a Sunday when school duties could

not interfere with the slow ritual of preparing the dinner. All five women came early in the morning. They helped me make the rolls, the salad, and the pie. They peeled the potatoes and shelled the peas. They watched me sear the roast. They helped me set the table—white tablecloth, linen napkins, candles. "A plate and fork to be used for nothing but the salad?" "Ah! A regular, standard, white-people dinner!"

A Tewa custom in Tesuque was that when invited to a feast, the guests stood outside the house door until a member of the household where the feast was given said in Tewa, "The food is ready. Come in. Sit down and eat." To say this in Tewa takes a long time and many, many words. Besides, Tewa is a tonal language and the tone in which a word is spoken gives it meaning. To use the wrong pitch could be disastrous. At the beginning of the year I had tried but I could not learn to give the right tone to the many—to me, meaningless—syllables.

So I had gone to the Council of Old Men and had proven to them that I could not say correctly the Tewa words, "The food is ready. Come in. Sit down and eat." This being true, I asked them if, instead of giving the Tewa welcome, I could ring the school bell when the food was ready. After a long discussion, they agreed that since I was a white person and did not know how to speak their language I could ring the school bell when the feast was ready to be eaten. For the first few parties I had to remind them that the school bell was my welcome, but after a while they accepted it. The ringing of the school bell meant that the feast was ready.

I talked this over with the five Tesuque women and explained that this time there would be no ringing of the bell. They would come at the hour of the invitation. If this was to be a dinner like white people had, then I would invite them for six o'clock, and when it was almost six o'clock they would start walking down the road to the school. Was that what they wanted to do? "Yes! Yes!"

I gave them an alarm clock. I set the alarm for ten to six. When the clock alarm sounded, they were to come. Did they understand? "Yes!" Would they do that? "Yes!"

At six o'clock my mother and a friend, who were living with me at Tesuque School, helped me put the food on the table. At seven, eight, and nine o'clock we waited. At ten o'clock we went to bed. The next morning the women came to the schoolhouse. They blew their noses and wiped their eyes. They put the food and the silver away. They touched the napkins and looked at the candles, and then put them away. No one spoke to me. I went about my work of teaching their children, who were very quiet and looked at me all day with storm-filled eyes.

Months afterward the women told me, "We were dressed, and so were our husbands, dressed for our party, and then we waited, but you did not ring the bell." "Did the alarm clock ring?" I asked them. "Yes, but you did not ring the bell." "But you said you would come when the alarm told you that it was time." "We could not come. You did not ring the bell to tell us that you were ready for us."

That could have been the reason. It may have been. I had not followed the custom of saying that the feast was ready for the guests. Ten guests who never came to dinner! Customs ignored can cost big prices, but I think it went deeper than my not ringing the bell. It took years of living with Pueblo people to make me realize that I had asked them to break a tradition.

This tradition has its roots in the fact that Pueblo Indians are a communal people. Their community is close-knit and the members are equal one with the other. For example: pottery making is a craft and is an individual undertaking; the potter can shape a pot, somewhat to her own liking, but not completely. The pottery of a certain village has shapes typical of that village. The potter can decorate somewhat to her liking, but not completely. She may use only her own designs or ones that have been given her. She can put a price of money on what she makes, and sell it, and the money belongs to her. But a *reward* for an act is different. No one person is *rewarded* for a special act. No one stands above the group.

Again I remember. I remember my young son spending weeks of Saturdays and Sundays training three Tesuque boys in a relay race to compete with another school. I remember the day of the competition and the aftermath of tears of my small boy coach. One of our boys was winning, but when he looked back and saw his village companions trailing him, he waited for them so they all could reach the goal together. No one stands apart as someone *better*.

Why did I not remember this when I planned my dinner party? For a small group to be rewarded by a dinner given by the teacher was not to be accepted. They might want it, might help to achieve it, but when it came to acceptance they could not do it. At last I learned. If I praised a child's accomplishments, a drawing, a poem, an examination paper, he threw it in the wastepaper basket, not in defiance, but in shame—shame to be singled out, either for praise or failure.

A teacher told me about something that happened to a boy she knew in an Indian pueblo where she was teaching. The boy had reached six years and his grandfather had come to ask her, the day-school teacher, if his grandson had not now reached an age to receive what was given to the other children. The teacher agreed that he was old enough, and it was decided that the boy was to enroll on the opening day of school. The grandfather was enthusiastic and the boy was delighted. Questions were asked. Forms were filled out. Everything was made ready.

According to his promise, the grandfather brought his grandson on opening day. The teacher, wanting to be friendly, said, "What pretty moccasins you have on!" Grandfather nodded in embarrassment; his child was being singled out. Then he looked at the other children and looked at his own boy, took him by the hand, marched him out of school and to his home. Nothing anyone could do would persuade Grandfather to send his boy back to school. In a year or two the grandfather died and the boy came to school, but over-age and resentful because he was behind his age group.

Years afterward, the teacher, still in the pueblo, coaxed the boy to tell her why Grandfather went home that day. The boy told her, haltingly, still ashamed, still hurt. His grandfather had spent days preparing him for school, buying him blue jeans, a red plaid shirt, a handkerchief, and a hat —but he had forgotten Whiteman shoes! His child was wearing moccasins when the others wore shoes. And then to be "singled out." That was hard to take. But to be singled out and fail—that was not to be endured.

Customs and traditions; traditions and concepts—these are the warp and the woof of the fabric of a people's culture. And to cut or to mar or to break one is to spoil the design and weaken the texture. I tell these things not to bewilder but to ask that white Americans recognize that other people have different values and different ways from those handed down to them and to ask that these values and ways be accepted with respectful minds and open hearts.

A teacher tells an Indian child, "Speak up. Speak clearly. Speak louder." To an Indian, the loud-voiced person can be termed a braggart. A teacher scolds a child and he laughs. In our culture a child does not laugh when he is scolded; that we call defiance. I had to live for years in South America and work with very primitive groups before I understood that with many peoples laughter is an involuntary reaction to any quick stimuli, like pleasure or fear or pain or grief.

Over and over I hear, "They are defiant." Perhaps it is not defiance. It could be fear. But even if it were defiance, what would you have them do when they know, and they know that you know, they cannot reach many of the goals that have been set up for them? What would you have them do—die? A part of them *does* die. And if it is defiance that they use, it is used that you may not know how much they suffer—dying.

I believe in discipline, I believe in orderly processes, I believe in respect for authority. But these are achieved by

35

inner growth. They are not things that can be added. We who work with children—parents, teachers, librarians, writers of children's books—are so fortunate because we can begin at the beginning by teaching acceptance through acceptance.

After my son was shot down during the Second World War, I could not bear, at least for a while, asking, as I had been doing, other young American pilots for Sunday dinner. I began asking Chinese cadets, training in this country, to have Sunday dinner with me. At this time I lived in a room at one of the faculty houses of an Indian boarding school. The room was comfortable, but I had nothing of my own in it. It was just a place where I needed to stay for a while.

For several Sundays the Chinese boys came, ate dinner with me, and were at ease and happy. One Sunday the school superintendent's wife asked them to tea. They were delighted to go, but when they went into her house they were embarrassed and miserable. Afterward they explained to me that this was a house of a most worthy scholar. Why did they think this? Why? Because one end of the living room in the superintendent's house was encased with books. Only scholars had books, and they were not scholars. A difference in values.

This reminds me of Valentino in Guatemala. Valentino was the only child in school who did not have shoes. It worried me, as the trailways and the market place seemed deep in filth and germs. I asked Valentino if he would like me to buy him shoes. Yes, he would like it very much. We went to the market. The child was in an agony of fear that the shoes would not fit, or the price would be too much, or I would change my mind. But at last he had the shoes. They fit. They were paid for. He put them on, knowing that they now belonged to him. Then—what did he do? He took them off, folded them in his poncho, and trotted off barefoot through the mud and the rain. Each morning he carried them to school, washed his feet at the schoolhouse *pila,* put the shoes on, and wore them in the classroom. But at recess time and at nighttime he carried them. Why? To me, shoes were protection for his feet. To him, they were a symbol of another way of life, not to be treated lightly, not to get muddied, and never, never to be worn out.

Another time at another Latin-American school I watched teachers grading achievement tests. After some of the children's names the teachers had placed code letters. When these children's papers showed high or even average competence the teachers were excited and the papers were gone over again with greater care. Explaining their excitement to me, the teachers said, pointing to their code letters after the child's name, "These letters mean that this child does not wear shoes. Imagine! His paper is good and he does not wear shoes."

Books. Shoes. We cannot understand such values, but we must learn to accept them. We expect children of other culture patterns to accept our traditions, our customs, our values. Why can we not learn to accept theirs?

In a government Indian boarding school a large number of young Navajo had been brought in from the reservation. These were older children who, for various reasons, had never been to school. This was their first experience. They were taught many new ways, such as living in a dormitory, eating in a cafeteria, attending assembly, and showing appreciation of entertainment by our custom of applause.

In a government Indian school the children attend the religious services of their parents' choice. The children whose parents said they were Catholic attended Catholic services. In honor of the school's opening the archbishop had come from some distance to say the Mass. There were flowers, candles, altar servers, and a choir. The children were impressed. As the Mass ended, they did what they thought would please the kind white people who had permitted them to come—they clapped and clapped.

There is no end to the stories I could tell you from fifty years of working with children and adults of other culture patterns. Stories that bring out the need of awareness of differences and their respectful acceptance, the need of loving communion between children and children, between children and adults, between adults and adults, between groups.

What can we do about it, we who work with people of culturally different groups? We can develop within ourselves the sensitivity of awareness, the patience for practice, and the willingness to learn to understand.

THREE

Our Southwestern Children

The American Southwest is rich in its children, who bring to it a wealth of different racial and nationality patterns, different root languages, different folkways, arts, crafts, games, literature, music, drama, and history. Nowhere else in the Americas is there such blending of slowly changing primitive patterns and rapidly changing modern norms. These are treasures of cultural heritage, and we should be mindful that they are treasures and cherish them. Our Southwestern land of desert and wasteland, mountain and valley, holds close to its heart three cultures—the Indian-American, the Latin-American, the Anglo-American.

Anglo-Americans, being the largest cultural group, look upon the people of the other two as separate minority groups. Members of the greater proportion of these minority groups have lower economic levels, poorer housing conditions, greater health and nutrition problems, fewer educational advantages, fewer work opportunities, and more serious language handicaps than most of their Anglo neighbors. We know these facts. We are concerned about them and want to help remedy this serious situation. We know, also, that many of these children come into our classrooms and our libraries frightened and confused, torn between two cultures—the dominant and the minority—two sets of standards and many different concepts and values.

However, I am not going to talk about these things. This would not be what I want my contribution to be. Rather I am going to remind you of the enrichment that each of us can enjoy if we permit these children to share with us their heritage and their potential.

I will limit my discussion to the Southwestern Indian-American children, but what I say about them I could say also about the Latin-American children, whose Spanish ancestors opened the gates of the New World for the Anglo to take, to have, and to hold.

Let me review briefly, quickly, the history of the Southwestern Indian-American. Millions of years ago these first people came walking into our country, carrying their possessions with them. The men's burdens were on their backs supported by tumplines across their foreheads. Their hands were free. They needed them free to use their darts, spears, and wooden clubs for protection, and for the killing of game. The women's burdens were on their heads or backs, freeing their hands for the gathering of plant foods along the trails. Their possessions were few—weapons, tools, utensils. What clothing they owned they wore.

These people came from northern Asia, a land bleak and barren and cold, at about the time that the fourth Ice Age was ending. At that time, probably, the Bering Strait was a broad land bridge and these people walked across it. Their movement was south- and eastward and extended over thousands of years. They did not come in mass migration but in small family-related groups, never numbering more than, perhaps, thirty people in a group.

These first people were primitive, simple, restless, having no organized government, no elected chiefs, no plan of settlement. They followed the rivers for fish, the animal trails for game, the fertile valleys for plant foods and seeds. They spread out over all the Americas, different groups at different times, settling in separate places mostly, but occasionally moving in among other groups.

There is no way of knowing how long it took a group to walk from northern Asia to our Southwestern land. One scientist made a chart showing that if a group walked steadily southward, moving its camp weekly, season after season and year after year, it would have taken seventy years. Seventy years of walking—walking! Old ones dying. New ones being born. What a people!

The slow centuries passed. More family groups came wandering into the dry and sunny land. They lived at peace with each other. They were seed gatherers, hunters of small game, fishermen—not warriors. Each group brought its own language. Each group knew how to kindle and use fire. Each group knew something about spinning hair, bark fiber, and grasses; weaving these threads into simple clothing, mats, and trays. They knew how to tan animal hides, make moccasins, animal-skin clothing, and fur and feather blankets.

Far to the south, in what is now Mexico, Indians had been experimenting in agriculture. Their first success was with corn. The cob was small and the kernels small and hard, each kernel in its own case. Slowly, by small migrating bands or perhaps by trade, the corn plant was introduced to the Southwestern Indians and they became a corn-growing people. After a time, squash and bean plants were brought up from Mexico and grown in the Southwest. The growing of crops changed the life ways of the people here. They wandered less. They built more permanent homes. Basket weaving was improved and the making of pottery was begun. Gradually, the related family groups moved closer together. They began to form group ways according to the resources of their environment and, as time went by, group culture patterns.

Again the slow centuries passed. Then an entirely different people came into the Southwest, settling near the groups who were already here. These strangers came also in small bands, each band having its own leader. They were a nomadic people, wandering about because they liked the life of nomads. They were fierce and warlike, fighters because they liked to fight. Little is known of their history. We think they may have come from Siberia, crossing at the Bering Strait and swarming in fairly large numbers over what is now Alaska and Canada. Before they drifted into the Southwest, they had divided into two large groups, calling themselves Apache and Navajo. This was several thousand years before the birth of Christ.

At the time of the birth of Christ all the Southwestern groups had developed life ways suited to their environment and needs. Some groups had built immense, many-storied houses of sun-dried bricks or hand-cut stone, sheltering a thousand or more people. Other groups were living in shelters less permanent but adequate for their climatic situation and their way of life. All groups had developed government, some more complex than others, and elaborate rituals and ceremonies of worship. They utilized all the wild plants of their region—cacti, yucca, hemp, water reeds, seeds, nuts, berries, fruits, and roots for food and medicinal purposes, soaps, dyes, clothing, and building materials. They grew crops of corn, bean, squash, pumpkin, and cotton, adapting their planting procedure to the regional types of soil, weather conditions, the cycle of growing seasons, and nearness to water. They were adept in the use of fertilizer, the conservation of moisture, and irrigation. Many of the irrigation systems of that time are in use today. These people were expert basket and textile weavers and molded and fired strong, durable pottery of pleasing shapes and designs. All of this was at its height in the first thousand years A.D.

Halfway through the next thousand years the Spanish came, the discoverers, soldiers, explorers, trailmakers, mapmakers, settlers. After another several hundred years the Anglo came, soldiers, explorers, hunters, trappers, traders, settlers. They fought, they conquered, they subdued the Indian groups, taking their forests and their streams. They killed their game. They changed their life ways. All this is history. History repeats itself. What was done to the Indian had been done many times before to conquered peoples by their conquerors. It will be done again. The story of people will go on and on as long as there are people. I recall this brief history of the Indians only to remind you of what they did, of what they developed, of what they had; what they gave to the people of today, and what they still have to give.

43

Today, Southwestern Anglo people value the barbaric splendor of the Indian ceremonial rituals. They value the strength of Indian art, the symbolism of Indian designs, the boldness of Indian color contrasts. They value the rhythm of Indian music, the beauty of Indian weaving and Indian pottery. But they tend to think of these things only as traditional, something that has been handed down from the past. They do not seem to realize that the shy, withdrawn Indian child has all the talents of his ancestors. He is a proud, shy, sensitive, creative person who, with only a little loving prodding, is capable of exquisite accomplishment.

Quite a few years ago, in the mid-1930s, at the United States Government Indian school in Phoenix, Arizona, the teachers experimented in fostering freedom of expression in the students' writing of their yearbook. The school enrollment included children from all the Indian tribes claiming Arizona as their ancestral home: Papago, Pima, Maricopa, the Colorado River tribes, the Hopi groups, Apache, and Navajo. Some of these children spoke English fairly well upon entering school, but there were many who came speaking only their tribal languages. The age range of these boys and girls was from ten to nineteen years. Some were up to age-grade level, but many were several years below. The children were given the opportunity to write anything they wanted to write; no topic assignments were given them. They were permitted to write and write and write. If, at last, they were satisfied with what they had written and if it had value in the opinion of their tribal peers, it would be included in the yearbook.

The teachers knew that the children were gifted in art and

the traditional crafts of their own tribe, but the discovery that they were deeply appreciative of nature and love of homeland and family, and could express their thoughts in simple and beautiful English, came as a surprise.

At random, I quote from the 1941 yearbook, which they titled *The New Trail*.

SLEEP

The sun goes down
and night falls.
Then I close my eyes
and go to sleep
in my bed under the trees.

PIMA BASKET

I am the Pima basket.
I was made of nature's materials.
I was once a willow standing by
the running water with the arrowweeds.
I was once a cattail waving in
the river with the fishes.
I was once a devil's claw growing in
the field with the squash plants.
I was once a pattern woven in a
legend of my tribe.
Now I am all these things
woven into one,
woven long years ago.

45

Now I am very old.
I am the proudest of my tribe.
I am the Pima basket.

PIMA LAND

Out in the sunlit West is the land of the Pima.
It lies beneath the purple arches
   of the sunset sky.
The singing of the wild birds,
   the crying of the wild animals
   ring through the air in this desert land.
The voices of the people,
   the sound of the drums and the rattles,
   the tunes of the native songs
   are heard around the campfire
   in the dark stillness of the night.
The mountains glow in the sunlight.
The lazy Gila River creeps slyly by
   on this ancient war ground of the Apache
   where the Aw-aw-tam now live in peace.

HOME ON THE WALAPAI

Here is the land where you will live.
Go to the place where the water is,
   mark off your land and live by the water.
Name the place where your home will be.
In summer live by berries and wild food.
In winter live in a cave on your land.
There you will have stored food,

food you had gathered in the summertime.
Give the land that you use a name,
a name like the Berry Patch
or the name of a river.

TRANSLATION OF A PAPAGO SONG

Singing alone,
Singing alone,
Here I am,
    singing alone.
Here I am.
Here I am, alone,
Running over here,
    running over here,
    dancing alone,
    dancing alone.

DEATH

Let it be, my father. You have left us alone in this world.
But go where you are headed for. Don't ever turn back to
    your children.
For there is only one trail that we can pass through.
Even though you've left us, we may follow you sometime
And meet you in the place called Y'ah-k'ah, ya [paradise].

PRAYER FOR RAIN

The prayer for rain
    is the prayer of the Hopi
    of the high mesa.

He prays for more rain
  from the beginning of the day
  until the end.
He prays for the sake of his crops.
And, if it rains,
  he will have fine crops.
His prayer is a great power,
  for the rain gods
  never fail to answer.
The Hopi prays for rain,
  the Hopi of the high mesa.

LONELY CALLS

How lonely and sadly
  the coyote howls
  at evening dawn.
All about the darkness creeps
  and the wise owls
  start to call.

WINDY DAY

High from a windy hill
  I see the swaying trees.
High, where I stood still
  on that windy day.

MOENCOPI

Cornfields grow green
  through the canyons of Moencopi.

Cottonwoods grow along the wash.
Cool breezes blow
  white clouds overhead.
The sun smiles with happiness
  through the canyons of Moencopi.

SONGS AT SUNDOWN

At sundown
  songs fill the air.
Songs of the men coming home
  from the fields at sundown
  through the green cornfields
  by the cottonwoods waving back and forth
  by the wash.
Songs fill the air
  at sundown.

SPRINGTIME IN MY RESERVATION

Am I proud to see my little reservation in the
  springtime, with the lovely cottonwood trees
  all around, and the smooth little road that
  leads to it?
In my childhood I lived there
  under the big cottonwood trees.
I saw the lovely sunsets, and the big mountains.
Oh, am I proud to see my little reservation
  in the springtime?
I am! I am!

My grandmother
likes to cook
for me.
I know
because she smiles
when she cooks.

I AM A PAPAGO GIRL

I am a Papago girl.
I live in a Papago village.
I am thankful for it.
It may be a dry, desert village,
It may be lonesome.
The sadness may cover me
but I am thankful for it
because I am a Papago girl.

THE DESERT

The desert is a lonely place,
it is lonely,
but I do not mind.
It is my home.
It is peaceful.
It is quiet.
It is beautiful.
The desert is a lonely place,
but I do not mind
because it is my home.

THE DAY IN THE DESERT

I love the morning,
   its cool dawning,
   its birds singing
   and the sun peeping out
   with its shining ray.
I love the noon
   with its stillness
   and its cool shades,
   yet the hot winds blowing
   in the desert sand.
I love the evening,
   its colored sunsets,
   its singing breezes
   and the cactus shadows.
I love the desert,
   its night birds singing
   in the bright moonlight
   with the shining stars
   of the night.

APACHE LAND

In Apache land there is a valley
   that comes from the southeast
   and goes on toward the west,
   along the sides of the mountain.
On the mountains, wild poppies bloom,
   green grasses grow and cattle graze.
Far below a silver stream is running.

I love this land where I was born,
This Apache land.

HAPPINESS

So let there be happiness.
We who live in this encampment
  here are poor.
We strive to live by the soil and
  labor of our hands.
So be on your way. And do not
  harm us.
So let there be happiness.

LITERAL TRANSLATION

Him sweetheart walking
he was singing
him I want
that's why I did
him I still want

FREE TRANSLATION

My sweetheart was walking.
He was singing.
That was why I walked with him.
He was singing.
That was why I walked with him.
I want to talk with him.
I want to walk with him
Some more.

Let us go up the road that
    leads into the blue sky.
Let us go up the road that
    leads into the blue sky.
Come, let us go up the road that
    leads into the blue sky.
There is a roan horse standing
    where everything is green.
There are snow-capped mountains,
    there are blue lakes, too.
The clouds are lazily drifting
    along.
This is the kingdom of the horses.

NAVAJO HAPPINESS SONG

Wherever I go, Wherever I go
Wherever I am there's happiness.
Dear, dear places I go
Dear, dear places I go
Wherever I go, Wherever I go
Wherever I am there's happiness.

This is what can happen to children when they are given
freedom to express their thoughts and encouraged by people
who care.

FOUR

Teach Them to Read

There is a file of papers near my desk captioned ANSWER
IMMEDIATELY! Today, looking through its tightly packed
contents for another "answer-immediately," I came across an
unanswered, forgotten clipping dated three years ago. The
clipping was a letter from a woman in Ohio written to Spud
Johnson for his column, "Gadfly," in the Santa Fé newspaper. This short letter from an unknown writer in an unfamiliar town in a state many miles away, about a small book
written more than thirty years ago, opened a floodgate of
memories of the many methods I have used to teach reading
to different groups of children I have known and worked
with along my way.

This clipping brought back memories of my first bout
with reluctant readers. They were reluctant, I thought then
and still believe, only because of the handicap imposed by
having to read in a second language before they knew how
to speak it with ease, understanding, and confidence. At the
time we teachers thought our lot heartbreaking because of
the almost impossible task that faced us every day. Now I
know these years were the richest of my teaching experience

and laid the groundwork for a lifetime of trying to bridge cultural differences.

These were the years when Willard Beatty was Chief of the Branch of Education, Bureau of Indian Affairs. He not only encouraged experimenting in teaching approaches and methods, he insisted upon it. For me, this was heaven on earth, and I experimented with gusto and delight. Many of my experiments were failures, but many were fruitful, and I accomplished many things before someone told me they could not be done.

But to go back to the clipping that opened the floodgates. It reads in part:

> Just recently I found a book at a church sale titled *A Courier in New Mexico* by Mabel Parsons. It was printed by the Tesuque Printers and inside its cover is a hallmark with the Tesuque Pueblo stamp. The book must be hand-bound for it is a different binding than what I'm familiar with. This book is divided into five sections and each section is preceded by what is obviously a hand-colored mimeographed map. The hand detail is unbelievable and I've wondered how any printer could do this and still stay in business. . . . Please let me know more about the Tesuque Printers.*

A Courier in New Mexico was written more than thirty years ago in the tiny Tewa Indian village of Tesuque. I was the Indian Bureau teacher for the one-room government day school. My young son, my mother, and my friend, Mabel Parsons, lived with me at the school and worked lovingly, unendingly, and unpaid with the Indian children and adults at the pueblo.

My son, my mother, and Mabel have made their last

* Reprinted from the Santa Fé *New Mexican*

journey along their life trails, but today, as I sit here remembering, all of us are back again in Tesuque as it was at that time more than thirty years ago. Each of us had many projects. The little schoolhouse was popping with ideas and activities, and the Indians, young and old, loved the excitement and came from early in the morning into the night to what they called "the much-working school."

Along with the projects there were also the problems. My biggest one was getting the four boys and one small girl (third-graders) to want to read "the books." They thought that books held the magic of all that they wanted to have and to be; but they also believed that this magic was somehow locked within the books' covers and only white people had keys that could open them. Since they themselves had no keys, they turned their small, stubborn wills against books and everything that had to do with books.

Experience Reading Charts were new in the 1930s, but all Indian-school teachers were using them to help in the teaching of English, their pupils' second language, and in teaching reading in that language to all the small Indians in all the government schools across the land.

Every day and many times a day at Tesuque the third-graders experienced experiences and then described them in shy, low-voiced, halting English sentences. They learned that these sentences could be written with symbols making letters and words and put by Teacher on a chart. These charts were illustrated joyfully by the children and, much to my dismay, memorized almost immediately and singsonged back to me. But these were charts, and to the children charts were charts and had no connection with books. I tried the next step of transferring the chart lesson to smaller folded-paper yarn-tied booklets. To the children these booklets were exactly what they were, pieces of folded paper written upon and tied together with yarn. They were not books, and the children still were against books.

There was nothing I could do but write a book about the things they knew and loved and were. This surely would prove to them that books are written by people for people to read and to enjoy. But to be accepted as a book, this book must look like a book with hard covers and printing that was not handwritten by Teacher. I had a hand-operated printing press that the mining company had bought for me when I taught in a mining-town school high in a mountain valley of the Pecos River. I had the right sizes and amounts of type, so we could print a book. But for illustrations we needed a mimeograph machine. The Tesuque day school had no mimeograph, no stencils, no mimeograph paper, no binding materials. As I remember, the mimeograph machine I wanted cost twenty dollars. Twenty dollars for a mimeograph machine for a day school in the 1930s! Not to be thought of! Mr. Beatty in Washington might want us to be creative teachers, but if our creativity cost money, the superintendent for the Pueblo Indian Reservations in Santa Fé was dead set against it. Each day school had an annual appropriation, but mine seemed mostly to be spent for toilet paper, mops and brooms, and yellow soap. There was little left for paper and pencils, picture books and textbooks, colored crayons and blackboard chalk. No money at all for a mimeograph machine, nor stencils, nor binding materials for a handmade book.

Mabel Parsons came to my rescue. She had been a Harvey Courier in the days when the Fred Harvey Company sold New Mexico by the busload-mile to eager Eastern tourists. Couriers had to answer all the questions asked them about New Mexico. Mabel, fresh from New York and loving New Mexico, had written down all that she knew so that she could read it quickly before each new tour. The manuscript was in a box somewhere; if she could find it, we could have it.

I remember the night she found it and gave it to me. Ideas came tumbling one over the other. We would buy the twenty-dollar mimeograph machine, using next month's grocery money; I could pay myself back before next month. We would buy stencils and the right kind of paper for printing materials and a book that would tell us how to bind a book. We would sell Mabel's book for a dollar a copy to pay me back for what I had spent. Mother was our bookkeeper; the expenses came to thirty dollars.

The book-hating third-graders with ceremony and pomp were henceforth the Tesuque Printers. They watched Mabel set type and ink it. They set each page on the disk and pulled the lever. Each time the disk came up and a printed page was removed there were excited exclamations—not in English, in Tewa. The classroom was strung with clotheslines on which the Printers tenderly put the pages of the book to dry. They chose a Tewa design for their hallmark stamp and hand-colored one for each book. There were five sections in the book, because there were five third-grade printers. Each printer was responsible for one section and for coloring the mimeographed map that preceded it. When the pages were dry and assembled, Mabel and the third-graders bound them. The second-graders were permitted to beeswax the sewing thread—they thought it a great honor.

At last the book was completed and sold. There were thirty copies and I was out of debt. But there were other results of *A Courier in New Mexico* that were of greater importance. The Tesuque Printers now knew that books were only sentences made by people and put on pieces of paper and sewed together. They knew how to bind books in hard covers and there were enough paper and binding materials left to make a new book about life every day in Tesuque, which by this time I had finished writing.

The new book we called *Third Grade Home Geography*. It was our book. The children had seen it written. It was about things they knew and they could read it. We made seven copies, one for each of the Tesuque Printers and one for the school and one for my mother, who had bought gay Indian calico for us to bind the books with. We used *Home Geography* for a year or two, but finally it got to Washington and someone there sent it to New York and *Third Grade Home Geography* became *In My Mother's House.**

Did the Tesuque Printers learn to like books? I do not know. They learned to read them and were up to age-grade level by the time I left Tesuque. I kept track of my five Tesuque Printers until all had finished at the Indian school in Santa Fé and had been sent on to other schools for added training, the boys to Haskell Institute, the girl, Veronica, to Riverside in California. Later, one of the boys went to college in California and another became one of the outstand-

* Published in 1941 by The Viking Press

ing members of the group of Indian artists in Santa Fé. Then the war years came and my trail way turned away from Santa Fé and the Pueblo Indians of the Rio Grande. I lost track of the little Tesuque Printers, and until today it had been years since I visited them even in memory.

Now that the floodgates of memory have been opened, I think of the many devices I have used in teaching children with a language handicap to understand and speak and read and write their second language. I have learned that there is not *one way*, but as many ways as there are children to teach.

For many years I was concerned only with teaching reading to children. I knew that many adult Indians, for a variety of reasons, had learned neither to read nor to write, but this seemed only to strengthen my resolution that this must not happen to children in my classrooms. I did not take the time nor the thought to realize that many adult nonreaders feel the need, the longing, and have the ability to learn to read and write in the language their white neighbors use so fluently and unceasingly.

I remember that I first recognized the tragic need for everyone to know how to read when I met one of the fathers of two children in my classroom. He was young, intelligent, outgoing, but he was blind. I still feel the sick rage I felt when I learned what had caused his blindness: He could not read, and, being too proud to ask for help in reading the labels on the bottles, he had used disinfectant in his eyes instead of the eyewash the doctor had recommended. It was then I realized that every man, woman, and child in our society has the need to know how to read.

So I knew the *need* for everyone to have reading skill, but it was not until years afterward that I was made to know the *longing* to be able to read that a nonreader may have. This happened in Guatemala, at a training school for rural teachers with a demonstration school for the near-by children. The occasion was a school fiesta of some kind. Its reason I have forgotten, but I remember a somber, stern-looking Indian bringing his small daughter to me and asking her to read for me. When she had finished, he said with pride, "The book talks to her." Then he took the book and looked at it for a long time. At last he spoke, and I will never forget the heartbreak in his voice as he told me, "The book talks to her but it does not talk to me."

I had not known before that people who could not read wanted to read. Now, with the realization of their need to read, I knew there was longing that for many people could never be satisfied.

At the Guatemala school we trained rural teachers for a period of three years, but before they could graduate at the end of the fourth year they had to spend a year teaching in a school with teachers who had not been trained by technicians from the United States. We did this purposely, knowing that if our teachers really believed in our instructional methods they could withstand criticism from teachers who did not believe in them. We thought it would be a waste of time, effort, and money to graduate teachers from our training school who had not this belief or, having it, did not have the courage to put it into practice. However, to make it more endurable for our teachers, we sent them in pairs, knowing that two can fight better than one. Most years the graduating class numbered thirty, but one year it was only twenty-nine. One teacher must go forth without a partner. A man by the name of Jemenez chose to be the extra one. He wanted, he said, to find a community that needed a school and him as teacher and to see what he could do with such a school.

In a highland village of Guatemala he found a community of five families whose children had no school to attend. There was no school building either, but Jemenez found an old abandoned two-room house. The roof leaked. The walls had never been painted. Under the accumulated dirt and rubbish of years, the dirt floor was found to be full of chuck-holes, but Jemenez was happy. He had a community and schoolchildren and a schoolhouse, if such a rubble could be called a schoolhouse. We offered to help him with the needed repairs. Jemenez said no. If the children wanted a school they would work with him to make it fit to be used.

I did not see them when they mended the roof, but I was there when the walls were being whitewashed. The children had dug gypsum, a kind of lime, glistening white, from a near-by cave of limestone. Their mothers had helped them mix it with water to the right consistency for putting it upon old board walls. Somewhere the children had found two boxes, a table, and a bucket. They were ready for their assembly-line procedure. The child on the floor lifted the bucket of whitewash to the child on the box, who in turn gave it to the child on the table. The table-top child held the bucket so the child on the box on the table could dip into it and smear the whitewash on the wall. The "brushes" were two homemade mittens of sheep wool. I knew the hue and cry that would be raised in many schools in the United

States at such a project, but this was not the United States. This was a country where the people's daily bread was labor and they felt that no price was too great to pay for the privilege of learning to read.

We offered to furnish Jemenez with school supplies, but he said no, they would make do with what they could find. The only supply he would take, and that reluctantly, was chalk for the blackboard that he and the children made. Made a blackboard? For Jemenez this was easy. He used curdled goat's milk, powdered limestone, and lampblack painted on one wall of the room. With the glistening white walls, the velvet black chalkboard, and the shining faces of the children, Jemenez' classroom was a place of beauty.

Almost as soon as the children had finished their classroom, they were reading sentences describing what they had done to make it ready. As each day's lesson was wiped from the blackboard the children looked in distress at the place where their reading had been and was now wiped out forever. We offered to give Jemenez chart paper and pencils and tablets. Jemenez said no, he would think of something. The next time we came to visit, each child had a wooden paddle for a tablet and used a bit of charcoal for pencil. Now the day's reading lesson need not vanish. Wood is cheap in Guatemala and so is charcoal. The paddles were placed carefully around the walls of the classrooms, treated with great respect and reread with pride.

Soon the parents came bringing gifts: boxes and pieces of boards for desks and benches and woven mats for the now smooth earth floors. Once when I was there they were building a brush shelter in back of the schoolhouse. When I asked them its purpose, they told me, "The teacher tells us that in your country of the United States there is a school lunch for the children. If such a happening should come to us, we must have a place where the teacher says school lunch should be served."

This is only half the saga of Teacher Jemenez. When the parents saw their children reading, they wanted to learn. When they had learned, they wanted to continue reading. There were no books in the village and only the priest received a weekly newspaper. He gladly gave it to the teacher, but the paper became torn and faded before all the people could read it. The second room in the made-over schoolhouse Jemenez called his office. The last time I was there the office walls were covered with pasted newspaper pages. Daily the people came alone or in twos or threes to read and reread and read again the miracle of the printed word.

There was Tito in a clearing in the brush in Costa Rica. To get to his school we went by plane, muleback, and dugout canoe. Tito had no books, but he had a substitute. He had pricked words on the broad, flat leaves of a jungle plant and the children were reading them, not as we think of reading, but it satisfied them. They were solving the mystery of the symbols of the spoken word and it gave them a sense of identity with a world they had heard about, but did not know.

Years passed. There came another turn in my trail way and I was given the work of training teachers in the preparation of materials for the beginning literate and the nonreading adult Indian in different parts of the United States. From the Mexican border to the Canadian line, wherever there were Indian reservations there were Indians who could not read, who knew their need, and felt heartache and shame because they could not do what others around them were doing. These people had the willingness and the ability to learn and, for the most part, they had strong and dedicated teachers. It takes dedication for a teacher in our country to live in a trailer far from a town, a railroad, a post office, to travel day after day to remote clusters of dwellings, and to do most of the teaching in the evening when the Indians' workday is over. We had such dedicated teachers. The Indians loved them and called them "our old men's teachers."

For every reservation and every old men's teacher, I could tell you a story that I can never forget and you would always remember. I will tell you only one. One to remember.

In one of the Papago villages in Arizona one summer evening when the heat of the day lay heavy and breathless across the stretches of sand, an old man came to the abandoned warehouse where we were holding classes. He came to look and to see, to listen and to hear. When the class was coming to an end he began to talk. Each teacher had an interpreter always at his side. The interpreter's instructions were clear and firm. He had to interpret everything that was being said as it was being said, but in moments of excitement the interpreter joined in the conversation with never a thought for the teacher who was imploring him to interpret. This happened when the old man began to talk. Everyone else began to talk, including the interpreter, each one trying to outtalk his neighbor in fluency and loudness. At last, when some conclusion had been reached and a semblance of quiet restored, the interpreter remembered the teacher. The old man, he said, had walked from his village, a distance of about five miles. He wanted the Santa Rosa people to lend their teacher and their building to his village people. The Santa Rosa people had told him that his people could come to their building and use their old men's teacher, but not on Tuesday or Thursday. They had learned to read "We come to school on Tuesday" and "We come to school on Thursday," they explained, and they were not willing to learn those sentences over again. They wanted a new reading lesson. It was decided that the other village people could come on Monday. Each Monday the old man was the first to arrive and the last to turn in his pencil and book reluctantly and trudge back through the darkness and the sand to his home five miles away. He was a slow learner but a determined one. I remember the last time I saw him in the borrowed schoolhouse. He had learned to write his name. He was waiting by the door when I came in. He asked me if I could write my name. I said yes, and he said, "Show me." I did, and then there was a pause until I realized what I was expected to say. I asked, "Can you write your name?" He answered yes, and I said, "Show me." He did, and as he held it up for me to see, his whole body trembled with the pride he was trying to hide. The next time I went to see him one of his friends told me, "He already dying." Then he added with as much pride showing as the old one had tried to hide, "But before he dying no more cross mark on paper for him. He writing his name good. Everybody seeing it."

Teach children to read so they will not have the heartbreak of being nonreaders in a world geared to reading. Teach the old ones to read. Teach them to read. There is the need. There is the longing. There is the willingness and the ability to learn. Teach them to write, at least their names, so that they will never again need to put cross marks instead of writing their signatures. Such small things can bring great pride and identity for them with their more fortunate neighbors.

FIVE

Seed of a Story

Again and again, people have asked me, "Where do you get the ideas for your stories, what makes you write them?" This is asked as a single question, but it has two distinct and separate answers. Answers that may be years, miles, places, peoples apart and have, at least on the surface, no relation to one another or to the final story which emerges.

The second part of the question is the easier to answer and, perhaps, the easier one for the questioner to understand. Why did I write a particular story at a particular time? The answer is simple. Some situation had begged to be probed, some need had demanded attention, some problem had called for a solution and so had to be written about. One or all of these reasons had caused me to write that particular book. This answer seems to satisfy.

"Seed of a Story" appeared in slightly different form in the 1964 *Thomas More Catholic Book Annual* © copyright 1964 by The Thomas More Association, Chicago, Illinois. Portions of the text here are from "Ships, Treasures, and Cargo," an address presented before the Texas Association of School Librarians, Galveston, Texas, in March 1962, and published in *The Texas Library Journal*, Vol. 38, no. 2, June 1962, and in *Top of the News*, American Library Association, December 1962.

But the first part of the question is the difficult one to answer. Where did I get the idea? Where did the seed come from? This cannot be answered automatically, without thought, without remembering, without deep digging into the mind to find the tiny seed that may have lain dormant for years, perhaps unrecognized, until a necessity found its planting place and a time seemed right for its growth. This small seed, more often than not, can be unearthed: the time, the place, the word, the act that gave it life-spark can be recalled with vivid exactness. But to explain this is difficult, because most often what comes forth in flowering bears little resemblance to what formed the seed.

I am reminded of the time, years ago—perhaps a quarter of a century ago—when I went to teach in a one-room day school in an Indian pueblo north of Santa Fé. I remember the place as I first saw it; the box-shaped mud houses, like children's blocks piled in uneven lines around the broom-swept plaza; the oblong fields encircling the houses and the blue-colored mountains cupping the whole in brooding, loving protection.

This was not my first Indian school, although in a sense it was my beginning as a teacher. For a year before entering the Bureau of Indian Affairs I was one of the teachers in an Indian boarding school in the pueblo of Zuñi. After entering the Bureau, I had taught for several years in a large non-reservation Indian boarding school, where I was one of the junior-high-school teachers. In both of these situations, problems had confronted me that I could not attempt to solve because I did not know what caused them or when they had become problems to the Indian children in my classroom.

I very much wanted to go to some small school where I could live close to the heart of the people, where I could get to know little Indians' first experiences with school and watch their development until they reached boarding-school age and were sent away from the pueblo hearthfire.

Surprisingly, although at the time I did not realize it, my wish was granted. I was sent to the Tesuque day school. In those days Tesuque was much as it had been for two or three hundred years. It was small, self-contained, and self-sufficient. The people were gentle folk, loving their home, their land, their traditions. They knew what life had been in the days of old—their ancients had told them. They thought they knew what its future would be because their ancients had left them the pattern. The white people, who were their neighbors down the dusty road on the other side of the river, disturbed them not at all. The Indian trail was a straight one and it was enduring. This, too, their ancients had told them.

The only change in the Tesuque way was the government school the white men in Washington had built for the Tesuque children. But the school, the Indians felt, was a comfortable distance from the village. What went on at the school need not affect the life of the pueblo, nor need pueblo life touch deeply the school hours of the children's day.

This was the thinking of the Old Ones at Tesuque Pueblo. What did the children think? I wondered, waiting.

The Council fathers came in a body to call on me. They came with great formality and dignity, but really not with much concern. If good came from having their children go to Whiteman's school they were for it. They would wait and see. "It has been said," they told me, "that Whiteman education will be good for our children. This might be true. If it is true, then you are to give this education to our young at once, quickly, in order that they may return without too much lost time to our normal Indian way of living."

This was the Council talking, the pueblo Old Ones. The children? What did they think? What did they want? I awaited the day for school to start. Then the children would come and I would know.

At last, first day of school arrived. I rang the schoolhouse bell. The children came down the dusty road under the giant cottonwood trees. They came with neither joy nor reluctance. They came as the Council had come, with formality and dignity, a handful of children, their dark eyes questioning but without much hope. They had been to school the year before, when it had first been opened. They had come all year, every day. Nothing had happened. They had confronted "education," but they could not capture it because they could not see it. But they knew where it lurked, and after a while they told me where it was. Timidly but knowingly they told me. It was in the books. It lived in the books. But how to get it out? Books were so difficult for them to read and so impossible for them to understand.

The days went slowly by and the patient brown-skinned babies sat looking at the books in awe and in despair. They did not understand a word they read. They did not understand the need for understanding. Books to them were not tools to know and to use. They were cages of power. They were Whiteman's medicine.

I tried everything I had been taught and everything I had learned along the way to show these poor little ones that books are things of worth only if we can understand what they say and we can learn to judge and use this knowledge. Gently I told them this in all the ways I knew. They looked at me with eyes that were dark pools of misery and that told me without words that here was something that I did not know.

Then one night suddenly a little seed of memory stirred into life. I was back again in Zuñi talking with a group of teen-age Zuñi boys. They were telling me of things that had happened to them, long ago, when they first came to White-man school. Idle chatter, or was it? Words have a way of living. Some talked with amusement and some with awe and some with a little hurt that still ached within their hearts.

This night in Tesuque, remembering, I could see them plainly, tall, quiet-spoken Zuñi boys. One of them was speaking, leaning against the wall, looking into the shadows, unaware of us who were listening. "This was the time they said we stole," he told us, laughing slightly to veil the little scar of hurt. "What we did had nothing to do with stealing, but how were they to know? We could not tell them how it really was." He laughed again, covering a breath of silence.

Then he told us the story. He had forgotten how many boys were in the group or how old they were. Numbers were unimportant. They had been in school for some time, long enough to come to the realization that there were as many things they did not know as there were feathers in the wings of the migrating birds. But the teacher knew these things.

Any knowledge they needed he could give them, and much that they felt no need to know he still could give them. Their awe turned to respect and finally to the desire to be like this One-Who-Knew-Everything. Where did he get this knowledge? What magic did he possess? They began watching him. Wherever he went they went. They hid behind bushes, around corners, watching his every move. They, too, would possess this Whiteman medicine when they could find out what it was. They did find out, and before long. Black Zuñi eyes see everything. The teacher had one habit that he never changed. Always and always he was putting his hand in his pocket, taking out a big silver watch, snapping it open, glancing at it, snapping it shut, and returning it to the safety of his pocket.

Aha! They had found the magic. It was caged in the round, flat thing of silver. They would have it for themselves. No more would they ever be thought slow-learning or little-learned. In a matter of days, the watch had disappeared. It no longer was safely in the teacher's pocket.

The calm of Zuñi boarding school was shattered and lay in sharp-pointed fragments in every nook and corner of the buildings. The teacher was irritated because his watch was gone. His white co-workers were indignant because a theft had been committed. The Zuñi Old Ones were furious because one of their own had broken a Whiteman rule. Unimportant though the rule was, breaking it had caused their Ancients to lose face. As for the boys, they were frantic. They could not find the magic. They snapped the silver cage open and shut until it would snap no more. Then they took the insides out. Every tiny screw and wheel they fingered and examined and tested. No magic. No medicine. Nothing.

The boy finished talking, then he laughed again. "Right then I learned," he told us, "that the head is a better place to keep Whiteman medicine. Since there was lots of room in mine I decided to fill it."

For a while all of us were quiet, each one thinking private thoughts. I remembered that mine had been grief for the hurt we give Indian children not knowing them very well.

This night, years afterward in Tesuque, I did not remember so much the hurt of having stolen something one did not steal. I remembered that magic is not enclosed in silver watches or clothbound books. But how to prove this to Tesuque children? We could tear a book apart, but all we would have when we finished would be tiny screws and wheels, words and dots and question marks.

But we could make a book. We could build it day by day from the things we knew. This would show the children surely that a book is only the keeping place for the things we know and understand and can use.

Thus the book *In My Mother's House* was written. It grew from the seed of a memory shared with a Zuñi boy who borrowed a watch to possess its magic. As it is written, it bears no kinship with watches nor with stealing. It bears no scar of a hurt of some Zuñi boys who stole something they did not steal. What came forth in the flowering bears little resemblance to that which formed the seed.

In My Mother's House was not furnished from the notebooks of the Tesuque children. At that time these children had no notebooks. They would not have known how to write in them or how to read them. It came not from their notebooks but from the things their hearts and minds could understand.

I am reminded of another time, another place, another seed that lay dormant for many years and at last came to harvest in the book *Santiago.**

On this day many years ago and many miles away I sat in the market place of a highland village of Guatemala, idly watching the kaleidoscope of changing colors and changing patterns of designs as the tiny highland women milled about, setting out their wares for sale. At first I sat without conscious thought or conscious feeling. Then I became aware that I was watching a baby being taught to walk. All the family participated in the instruction, father, mother, old grandmother, a teen-age boy. Each one was intent on the baby's efforts, serious, patient. The child was given no support of any kind, no touch of comfort, no loving word. Each time the baby fell the nearest one picked it up gently and quietly put it on its feet again, placing a folded square of cotton on its head. I suddenly realized that this baby was not only trying to balance its body with its first steps, but in addition to body balance it had to learn to balance a burden on its head. As I sat there watching, I thought of many things.

I thought of all the women I had seen, running along the dusty roads with a paddling movement of arms and shoulders, carrying on their heads their basket burdens. It might be a fifty-pound sack of flour or a basket full of live turkeys

* Published in 1955 by The Viking Press

or a pyramid of eggs or fruits or vegetables. When trains stopped at wayside stations the women came running from houses hidden from sight by vines and trees. They came swiftly, laughing, each one wearing jauntily her basket-burden crown. The train passengers crowded to the car windows to look down, choosing hot tamales in banana leaves, hot coffee in a granite pot, milk in a glass, sugar in a bowl, with never a drop or a grain or a crumb spilled from the flat basket tray atop the glossy, braided hair.

I remembered the men I had seen jogging up and down the steep embankments along the country roads, carrying loads of incredible weight in woven shelved crates, not in their arms or with their hands but resting on their backs and tied to their heads by leather tumplines around their brows. If all their wares were sold and they had bought nothing to replace them, they put rocks in the crates to carry on the homeward trail because they had been taught to balance their bodies with their burdens.

Later on I came to know small Valentino, happy, intelligent, alert, who wore shoes, carried his books in his hands, and was learning to read. I knew and loved his parents and was always welcome in their clean, swept hut in the clearing. They were burden bearers. This was their life. It was all they aspired to for themselves, but for their son their dream was for a better life.

The years passed, but the thought kept with me. What happens to the burden bearers' children who dream of a life of working for wages in the towns? The generation that breaks away from the home trail and is not quite at ease nor quite accepted on the sidewalks of the town must have shed many drops of bitter tears and precious blood along the road between.

So another seed had been planted, watered with caring, and the book *Santiago* thrust its plant leaves through the soil of memory. We gather the seeds of stories at random along the trails we tread, and we never know from the size of the seed what the shape of the leaf will be.

This happened in Zuñi many years ago, but I remember it as if it were yesterday. Zuñi is one of the largest Indian pueblos in New Mexico. Its houses are of adobe or of stone, flat-roofed, box-shaped, crowded together on the hill upon which the village stands. Between the groups of houses are narrow, crooked passageways that twist and wind by high-walled patios and lead to small hidden dance plazas.

On this day that I remember, children played in the sun that shone down warm and bright on the sandy banks of the trickling Zuñi River. Young girls in bright-colored shawls, carrying their water jars on their heads, swiftly climbed the ladders to their second-story pueblo homes. Young men walked by, going somewhere, or leaned against the house walls dreaming of the future. Old men, huddled in their black blankets, sat in the sun, dreaming of the past. There were the sounds of wood being chopped, of barking dogs, of muffled drum beats, and of someone singing. Smoke from a hundred cooking fires curled upward like lazy fingers writing on a blue-slate sky.

Modern, normal, peaceful—an Indian village winding up its work of the day—or so it seemed on the surface, but below the surface of everyday affairs, there was something stirring. Even I, the stranger, could feel it stirring. There

77

was a tenseness, an expectancy, a waiting. A waiting as the old pueblo had learned to wait centuries before the birth of the Christian Christ.

Beneath the surface of the smooth, hard-packed earth in the plaza, above the honeycombed hill that lay under the houses of Zuñi, something was happening. In the secret, sacred, smoke-filled, shadow-filled underground ceremonial rooms, something was happening. A rite unchangeable, unbreakable, slowly, slowly was performed. An ancient dance fraternity, one of the oldest, the most symbolic, the most ritualistic of all the secret fraternities of Zuñi was making ready for its public ceremony in one of the dance plazas of the village above.

I knew about this dance because I knew one of its dancers. She was a young student in a government boarding school. She was bright, happy, gay—not unlike any dark-haired girl in any school across our land. But suddenly she had changed. She had become withdrawn and had kept to her room in the school dormitory.

The weeks wore on. Finally she confided her trouble to a trusted teacher. She belonged by clan and blood and heritage to the age-old Zuñi secret fraternity of Those-Who-Swallow-the-Sword. There were now only a handful left to carry on the ancient, proud tradition and the strict and patterned ritual. She was the youngest one, the one who had been away, who had seen the other side of the mountain. Perhaps she had substituted new beliefs for old ones, new skills for those she had perfected as a child.

When very young, she had begun training in the rites of the fraternity, but school had taken her away. Now she feared that she had forgotten what she had been trained to do. She was afraid. She was afraid to thrust a foot-long sword of sharpened wood down, down, deep into her throat in the prescribed manner and for as many times as the ancients had set the pattern. She had not chosen to belong to the fraternity. Her clan, her blood, her heritage had called her to its membership. Now she had almost forgotten that she belonged to Those-Who-Swallow-the-Sword.

It had been a long time since the fraternity had given its public ceremony, but it was giving it this year, and those who belonged were compelled to take part. Someone had said to her, "You are one of us. You have been one of us since you were born. You will be one of us until you die. This thing that we do, we do because we must. You, too, must do it—our ancient ones demand it."

And now she was here in Zuñi, the schoolgirl from the government boarding school. Her sweater with its letter on the sleeve was packed away. Her high-heeled slippers were packed away. She had come to take the part that destiny decreed she take. In the mystic, secret ceremonial room she, with the other dancers, was being made ready for the ritual.

The hush in Zuñi grew tense. The silence grew heavier. It could be felt. It almost could be touched. Excitement rose, wave on wave on wave, more forceful perhaps because it was surrounded by silence.

The sun set slowly behind the gray hills, leaving a sky of red and gold. The people came swiftly, quietly. They came from the river. They came from their gardens. They came from their fields, from their houses. They poured into the narrow passageways, a living stream of color. They stood

79

three-deep against the house walls, black-blanketed men, bright-shawled women. They covered the rooftops of all the houses around the small dance plaza. No sound was heard except the soft swishings of blankets and shawls.

Then came the dry, rasping sounds of notched stick against stick, bone against bone, as the chorus of old men entered the plaza. They did not sing. They had no drums, no whistles, no rattles. They made no music, only a rhythm of stick against stick, deer rib against deer rib, that was force and power and mystery made into sound.

The dancers entered the plaza. There were ten men dancers. Their kilts were black, and eagle plumes were tied in their long black hair. There were five women dancers in handwoven black ceremonial dresses. Black bangs covered their faces, and eagle plumes were tied in their hair. In their right hands the men carried rattles, the women, two eagle feathers. In the left hand each dancer carried a sword of juniper wood as long as his arm from elbow to fingertips, the handle topped with feathers twice as long as the blade. The juniper sword was as wide as the dancer's thumb and ended in a rounded point.

Of the five women dancers, four were old and one was young. Their feet scarcely touching the ground, their dance steps were perfectly timed with one another and with the patterned sound of the old men's chorus. With each high step their bodies swayed in unison, their heads thrown backward, their left arms raised, a jerking movement upward. Grasping the sword by its feathered hilt, each dancer thrust the flattened, pointed piece of wood deep, deep into the throat, in and out, to the rasping sound of stick and bone.

The first in the line of dancers, the young one, was the girl who had been so filled with terror. She led the other dancers around the plaza, around and around. If she missed a beat, a step, a movement, the others would follow. If her throat refused to accept the sword, death would be sweeter than the wrath of the ancient gods that would descend upon her.

I was afraid to watch her, and yet I could not take my eyes away. I knew her in the classroom. I had seen her playing basketball. I had heard her sing in glee club. Now I watched as she performed a mystic ritual of an ancient people. Why was she doing this when she was afraid to do it? I do not know. We are never told these things. Did she believe in something that I could not understand? I do not know. I know only that she was afraid and that she had a right to be. I know only that she was there in the dance plaza doing that which she had to do.

I tried to build upon this memory when I wrote *Santiago,* a story of a boy who faced two worlds, who was not certain that he belonged in either of them.

Again, I am reminded of a day of many years ago. It was my first Sunday in the little Indian village of Tesuque, which is among the smallest of the Indian pueblos of New Mexico. It lies sheltered in the foothills of the Sangre de Cristo mountains of the Rockies. It lies within itself and in its past. It looks backward into tradition for its rules for the future. The old people and the old ways are stern and unbending. Yet it knew the meaning of tolerance.

On this Sunday noontime my young son and his cousin had gone exploring the new and exciting land that now was theirs. They came back much sooner than I had expected them, their arms loaded with what, they explained, had been a wonderful find. "Look at these old pottery jars and at all these bunches of feathers just thrown around on a kind of little hill," they told me.

My heart sank. Looking at them, I knew that the old pottery jars were sacred vessels. The bunches of feathers were sacred prayer plumes, and the little hill was a sacred Indian shrine. My boys, not knowing what they did, had desecrated a holy place.

So we went before the Council of Old Men, my boys and I, bringing the pots and the feathers. I told them what my boys had done. They showed the old men the things they had found. The Old Ones sat in a half circle facing us and our sins. They were stern, deliberate, detached, apart from me. They did not talk together, but I felt a communion among them in which I did not share, one in which I was not allowed to participate. We sat for a long, long time. Suddenly the communion flowed outward, taking us into its thought stream. Somehow I knew that we had been judged . . . and forgiven. At last, the oldest man spoke, "We have thought about this thing that has been done," he told us. "We have decided that it is all right. There are so many things that you cannot be expected to know."

From this one memory I have tried to build many stories that have to do with tolerance—the need to be able to accept, the need to be accepted, the gift of understanding, the need to be understood: the Herder books, *Little Navajo Bluebird,* my plea for teachers to understand small Navajo children. Although I really wrote those books for teachers, it is the Navajo children who seem to love them.

World Song tries to picture the terrible loneliness which engulfs one when there is no communion with fellow men and how one simple heartbeat in common, one mutual enthusiasm, can become a bridge for strangers to cross. In *Secret of the Andes* and *Looking-for-Something* I built upon the universal need to have and to hold a loved one, a home place, a place in a heart and in the sun. *In My Mother's House* attempts to convey the absolute delight in the security of being a part of some established thing.*

There are other seeds I have gathered along the edges of the trails I have walked that have not yet thrust plant leaves into the sunlight of recorded stories. I have watered them with the tears of my heart and cultivated their seedbed with the toil of my hands. Perhaps I may never see the glory of their blossoming, but they will live forever in my treasured memories.

A cold night on the Navajo reservation—the last night of a Navajo curing ceremony. Flat gray wastes of night-shadowed sand, flat gray expanse of cloud-heavy sky. From miles away through dry sand washes, over dry sand dunes, around the jagged red rocks, from within the hidden canyons, The People have come, by wagon, by truck, by horseback. The fires glow and smolder and glow again as a fretful night wind

---

* *Little Navajo Bluebird* was published in 1943, *World Song* in 1960, and *Secret of the Andes* and *Looking-for-Something* in 1952, all by The Viking Press.

sweeps across the wastelands. The smells of burning piñon and cedarwood, of fried bread and roasted mutton, of coffee boiling and tobacco smoke mingle with the smell of people, the smell of sheep waiting to be butchered, the smell of sweating horses, tired after weary miles of travel, and the crude, raw stench of gasoline and exhaust from an over-heated truck.

In the night shadows, the Old Ones visit, catching up on news of absent clansmen. Young men sing, children play, and women cook.

Inside the high dry-branch enclosure, a sick woman sits by the side of death. Her face is drawn with suffering, her eyes alive with pain. Her thin claw hands are clenched, her bony knees drawn up. The medicine man, detached, mysterious, works over her, making magic with incantations, chants, symbolic gestures. His medicine pouch is holy to him. His medicine is holy to him—dust of red earth, a shell, a splinter of bone, wing feather, and claw. He moves with majesty. He moves with serenity. He moves with assurance. He sees the people who have come to partake of the good he releases. He sees the sick woman who sits with death. He hears the bleating sheep in the night corral—his payment for this cure. For there will be a cure. The woman will live. She has faith in the power of the medicine man. Her faith will sustain his medicine. Faith!

Or choose this memory if you will—in the dry-parched land of the pueblos, where the sky is empty of cloud or even of promise of rain. The *acequias* are dry. Mother Ditch has no water to give them. The dirt of the plaza is hard and cracked. Heat haze veils the mountains and whirlwinds turn on the banks of the dry arroyos. The corn droops in the fields. The children are listless and quiet—no older people are in sight.

Then from the kiva comes the sound of drums; comes the sound of rattles; comes the sound of pebbles in the dry gourd shell. People come from nowhere and everywhere. They fill the plaza, leaving only enough space for the chorus and the dancers.

The old men walk into the plaza. Their drummer leads them. They stop at one end, with the drummer in the center of their circle. The line of rain dancers comes into the plaza, dancing the steps that have been handed down to them by their forebears through the generations and the centuries. The old man pounds his drum with the flat of his hand and the singers chant to its pounding.

The dancers pound the earth with the flat of their feet and the earth vibrates to their pounding, to the pounding of the drum and the chanting of the singers. Deep in the heart of the earth the pounding begins and comes up into the world of men. You can hear the pounding, you can feel it. It enters through your skin. It presses against your body. It sits in the pit of your stomach. It hits against your eyes.

The chanters chant the age-old chant, "Bring the rain. Bring the rain. Bring the rain."

The heavens open. The rain pours down, bathing the people in a life-giving refreshment of their faith. The people's faith—and you, who have no faith in rain making and rain makers, go home exhausted and yet refreshed, an emptiness within you and yet a feeling of having been renewed, reborn.

In memory, I walk again in the ruins of the white-walled city of Cuzco in Peru. Its walls seem whiter than the snow peaks around it. Its walls seem more enduring than the jagged rocks of the Andes that tower above the walls of the city, piercing the sky. The builders of this great ruin have gone the trail of no-returning, leaving little that lives behind them excepting the glory of their faith that is as alive today as it was a thousand years ago. The glory of a faith that built the city and that still fills the walled ruins, blessing the unbelievers as well as the ones who had been chosen to believe.

Down the Andes mountains, in the Valley of Cuzco, is the great circular stone where the Inca holy ones chained the sun in solstice. They believed they had done it to the god they worshiped, the all-powerful Sun. The Inca are gone. We still have solstice—and who are we to know what power the faith of a primitive people had in a primitive world?

Each little town of the Andes has its imposing Christian church, where the walls are covered with gold leaf and hung with tapestries embroidered in threads of gold and encrusted with jewels—and the people in the town go without bread.

At first these things appalled me, but not any more—not after I have seen these people go on their knees before the altars of their God. I have seen their faces. I have seen their eyes lifted. Their churches are the only beauty in their lives. Their faith is the only bread that can ease their hunger.

In Chichicastenango, I have watched the humble highland people go into their churches as into the home of a friend. I have seen them bring their gifts, first fruits of their gardens, to offer to Him as their small gift. I have watched them make mosaics on the church floor, mosaics of corn kernels, corn pollen, petal, and seed; each mosaic lovely to look at and lovelier in symbol. These people are burden bearers, humble, self-effacing, sad, but when they talk to their God, their faith in Him so raises them in their own estimation that they feel truly in His image and His likeness.

In northern New Mexico the people bring their crippled loved ones to the Church of the Black Christ at Sanctuario. In Guatemala they bring their lame, their blind to the Church of the Black Christ of Escupulo. The images are identical. The carvings are alike. The wood is the same. Age has discolored the two figures of the tortured Christ to the same soft blackness. The Christ of Escupulo is the older image by many hundred years. The one in Sanctuario must have been copied from the older one. Who took it to New Mexico a hundred years ago? Who carried it those impossible miles through jungle and rain forest, across mountain range and swampland? Who walked by foot over a trailless land bearing the large and heavy crucifix of Christ upon his shoulders to bring it to a people strange in blood and customs but akin in faith?

These are the seeds of many stories—courage, tolerance, and faith.

SIX

Challenge and Responsibility

All writers have something within their minds and hearts that urges and compels them to write. They feel some force that beckons and entices them to write. It is a necessity to express themselves, to explain their own beliefs, to answer their own doubts. Some call it the writer's challenge.

Each writer has his own particular kind of challenge. Perhaps for some writers the challenge changes according to circumstance, situation, or mood. This is not true for me. For me the challenge is always the same. It is unchanging. The challenge that urges and pushes, forces and compels me to write is *need*. It is the need that I think exists for the kind of books I try to write.

This need, I believe, is for children to have books written for them that will help them develop an understanding of themselves, their potentialities and resources, and the pressures and problems of their immediate world. It is the need for books to be written that will help give them an insight into, and an acceptance of, the larger world outside their own.

When I was a child my immediate world was safe and

small. Its boundaries were rigid and tight and strong. The outside world was vast, limitless, faraway, and unknown. It scarcely touched my life. It did not give me great concern.

This was true at the time of my childhood. It is not true today.

Today, a child's immediate world is one of ever-widening circles, moving outward, engulfing all that but yesterday was unthought of and unknown. The world outside has grown smaller. It has come nearer, it now lies but a step beyond our dooryard.

If our children are to be a part of this new world with any measure of harmony and confidence they must have knowledge of what today's world is and what it holds. They must know that there are other life ways, standards, and values besides the ones that we have taught them. They must know that other people are apt to act and react according to the pattern of their own traditions and cultures.

Our children need a measuring stick of larger dimension than the one which was adequate several generations ago. Children need to know children of other nationalities and races so that, inheriting an adult world, they find a free and joyous interchange of acceptance and respect among all peoples.

One way for our children to know these things, to gather this knowledge, is from the books that are written for them.

This, then, is my challenge—to add my bit to the books that I think should be written. This, then, is the light that beckons. I try to follow it, not changing my course, not looking toward greener pastures, but plodding along, book by book, using the gifts that have been given me to use.

What must these books have, if they are to be true to the pattern of the people in them?

I believe there are five qualities that such books must have. These qualities are aside from interest, achievement, and maturity levels. They are aside from plot, suspense, and style. They do not form a framework upon which to hang a story: They are the core of its being.

There is the quality of honesty. A writer must believe in what is written. There must be sincerity in what is said. The story picture must not be distorted. It must be as the writer sees it. The truth must not be disclaimed. It must be as the writer believes it. A writer must be true to the world and the people he writes about, and they in turn must be true to themselves.

A writer must not be tempted to mold the characters in a story to a pattern of popular conception, to what he thinks his readers want or to what he thinks they believe should happen. A writer's task is to create people that are as real as he can make them and to create situations that are typical or at least plausible in the lives of these people. It has been my experience that, given these two things, the writing is honest writing.

The people in books must be true to what they are. I believe this. I try to follow this. If I am writing about an Indian child, I want him to be an Indian. I want him to be true to his Indian kind. I want him to be those things that I believe are Indian. Indian tribes differ and Indian individuals differ, but in the main there are certain characteristics that are common to all Indians.

There is a slow-moving deliberateness in thought and

action. An Indian is slow to change. There is a certain quality of majesty that through the years of history has remained strong and dominant. An Indian may have inner confusion as to his own place in the white world, but he never doubts the power and the glory of his ancients in the Indian world. There is a oneness existing between the Indian and his Indian world and a sense of loss and frustration if that oneness has been put aside or sacrificed. These things are true of Indians in life. They must be true of Indians in stories.

If I am writing of children of Spanish-American heritage, I want them to be warm-hearted and gay, tender and sensitive. These people tread lightly over their life trail, and even in the shadowed parts there is always a sunray to warm and comfort them. Although many of them live close to their Indian neighbors, they do not live close to the heart of the earth as their Indian neighbors do. Rather do they live lightly, happily on its surface, and yet they are so deeply rooted in their own traditions that they can make any acre of land Old Spain within a generation span.

Many of the Indians and the Spanish-Americans have the same environment. They live under much the same conditions. They face many of the same problems, but their reactions, their values, their tempo of life are different. So must my books portray them.

A writer is only a writer. He can give only what he is capable of giving. He is not infallible, but he can and he must be honest.

There is the quality of accuracy. The information that the writer gives must be correct. He must check and recheck.

He must look and listen and, if at all possible, he must have done what he says has been done. His sources must be reliable and of different points of view.

My most comfortable writing is about what I, myself, have experienced. If I say that the rain-forest trail was heavy with the wet smells of growing things, I want to be able to recall those smells as I write about them.

If I write of a sandstorm on the Navajo reservation, it helps me to remember a time there when sand covered the desert world and all within it in a thick, yellow, choking, suffocating blanket, and the wind cried in desolation as it flattened the desert bushes, beat in fury against the cliffs of red rock, and blew the road away.

If I write about a forest trail, I want to know what was growing by its side that certain month and day my story children walked it.

If I write about these things, I want to hear again the silence of a desert noontime and the soft murmurings, the low calls, the winged rustlings, and the padded footfalls of a jungle night.

I want to know how the winter pine trees look when the frosted snow bedecks them in jewels and the morning sun brings forth the glory of their luster.

I want to have heard the swallows sing their rain song and to have seen a tree heavy with iridescent blossoms and, at a sound, see those blossoms take wing in warbler flight.

This gives me comfort in what I write. *You* may not have seen or heard these things. They may not have happened to *you*. But if they happened to me, I feel security if they happened to the children I write about.

92

However, it is not possible to have experienced all that one wants to write about and research must take over. There must be no counting of the endless hours of research time. I recall that for one book it took the greater part of a week for me to find out the kind of springs there were on a coach of a certain date and make. Such a minor thing as making certain how much the riders bounced as their coach rolled along took on major importance for the accuracy of knowing what *Father Kino* felt on the first days of his journey to the New World.

Even with the most careful research there happens now and then some sort of misinterpretation, a reading between the lines, something that lessens accuracy and thereby weakens the tale.

In many of the books I write, experience alone is not enough. Research alone is not enough. There must be a blending of the two. I give the example of *Medicine Man's Daughter.**

I am Southwestern. I was born on the periphery of Indian country. All my life I have gone to Indian ceremonial dances, dances for rain, dances for fertility, blessing and curing dances. I know these dances; as the Spanish say, "I know them as I know the palm of my hand." And yet when I had need to write about the great Navajo curing ceremony of the Mountain Chant, I had to spend hours in research. Did the sand painter take the sand in a handful and sprinkle it sparingly or did he take it between thumb and forefinger? Would a young girl, in training as a medicine woman, be allowed to do some certain thing? These questions had to

*Published in 1963 by Farrar, Straus & Giroux

be answered by seeing again, by asking those who knew, by reading pages and pages of old chronicles and modern writings.

It was the same with the country itself. I have traversed the Navajo country for probably fifty years. I have bounced over its rutted sand roads in truck, jeep, and car. I have flown over it in a small two-seater plane. I have walked along its trails. I have camped in its sand wastes and canyons. I have taught its children.

But when I wanted to write *Medicine Man's Daughter* I had to go again to Canyon de Chelly and sit for hours on the edges of its deep rock sides. I had to see its dawns, its sunsets, its starlight and sandstorms. Then I had to check maps, diaries, history books. What comes out? A small book of perhaps only passing interest. But to me it was a part of my life while I wrote it. I lived it with the people in the story. When I was finished I felt a sense of loss because these people had passed on out of my life, never to be met quite like this again.

There is the quality of reality. To my mind a book about people must be filled with the things that happen to people. Some of these things may be happenings of great suspense or drama, which is good if these suspenseful and dramatic events are probable and possible. But many happenings do not have these dramatic qualities, yet they make the framework of our lives and we should be made aware of them and their dearness because they are part of our every day.

A book about people should be made up of laughter and

tears, joys and sorrows, and the peace of all the humdrum hours, because that is what life is made of.

On the other side of the mountain there *can* be, but there need not be, bandits in hiding, lost treasures waiting to be found, villains filled with gleeful malice, or damsels in distress. But there need not be these things. Instead, there can be—just the other side of the mountain, the adventure of having reached there and the prospect of return. These things are real. They happen to us every day. It should be refreshing to know that they happen to other people, even to the people in the books.

Sometimes I have the feeling that we are leaping from suspense to suspense. And where can it lead us? Only to violence. I make a plea for recognizing and enjoying the small, simple realities of life.

Why is it not enough to waken with the anticipated joy of being alive for all the day? Do we need to tell our children that each of us must kill our daily dragon? Dragons can be fun. It is good to have them now and then. But as daily fare they are not reality.

I feel the same way about birth and death. Birth is such a natural event that we seldom stop to think of its magnificent miracle. The blossoming of life in tree and flower or any other living thing is something that should be read about by every child. It is the greatest miracle that we can experience.

In the same way, I feel that death should be met in books. Death is not black magic. Our children should not shun or fear it. The person who dies has new rebirth. Only to those who are left behind are there tears of pain. Books can show children that this is true; that tears are for ourselves and not for the departed ones. Children are not spared from having death touch their lives. Death happens on every side. It is a part of living. They must be taught to face it.

Let us lead them gently and in beauty to face reality. It must be faced.

There is the quality of imagination. There must be imagination in writing. Blessed is the writer with a rich imagination. Blessed are the books he writes for they yield a fruitful harvest for the children who read them.

The writer with imagination makes his own pictures with the words he writes. They can be bathed in beauty, etched in vividness, filled with power, consoling, promising, compelling. We make our pictures with our minds and hearts, our wisdom, our experiences, and we paint them with delicacy or with boldness from the nouns and verbs, adjectives and adverbs that we keep in our writing paintpots.

For every picture that a writer paints, two pictures emerge: the one that the writer makes; the other, the greater, the one the reader is able to fashion from the words he sees on the printed page. He paints them in the image of his own experiences and colors them with his own hopes and visions and dreams.

Imagination—the power of forming pictures in the mind. Our children need to be confronted with this kind of writing. They need it as escape from the harshness of life experiences, from the heartbreak of problems that they cannot solve, from the confusion of living upon the edges of an adult-pressured world.

As we look backward we cannot count the times when the

magic of imagination has lifted us from the black pools of despair, has comforted us with a brief moment of escape, has fitted us with hope, has given us stronger wings for longer flight.

If a book is to have value, it must make pictures of the people in the book, of their life ways, of their hopes and fears, their failures and their triumphs. Children make their own interpretations of these pictures in their hearts and in their memories. If the memories are vivid enough they will become a part of every reader's fund of knowledge, of his preparation for changes that he must face, and, perhaps, of his beliefs and his values.

But imagination must be strongly built upon honesty, upon accuracy, upon reality.

There is the quality of appreciation. There must be appreciation in writing. Books for children should help develop an appreciation of life and all that life means and holds and promises.

Books should foster an appreciation of beauty. There should be appreciation of the earth that lies around us, of the empty or cloud-filled sky, the peaceful rivulet, the restless sea, the awesome, majestic mountaintop, the sunlit plain.

But appreciation of beauty is but one appreciation.

There should be an appreciation of fear and the courage it takes to face it and the bravery to combat it. There should be an appreciation of joy and sorrow and the knowledge that one could not be as great without contrast with the other.

If children are to live fully, they must have full appreciation. If they have experienced vicariously hate and love, cruelty and compassion, greed and generosity, they will be better fitted in life to recognize, to weigh, and to reject those things that foster weakness and to take for their own those that foster strength.

Children should be given an appreciative awareness of the small things of every day. They should appreciate greatness, of course, great things, great events, great people. But great things have a way of drawing attention to the greatness of what they are and what has been accomplished.

Small things are apt to lie unnoticed in our treasure chest of time, and yet it is the small things that make up the bulk of our days. If we do not appreciate them we may live in poverty and die impoverished and never know what richness, what beauty, what good lies unknown, uncared for, unappreciated just beyond the reach of our hands.

I believe that children need children's books that have been written with honesty, accuracy, and reality. They need books that develop deeper understandings and broader acceptances, that enrich imagination and foster appreciation.

Their need is my challenge. Satisfaction for this need is my responsibility. This is what I believe.

SEVEN

What Is a Book?

What is a book from the writer's viewpoint? It is a part of the writer's life, his beliefs and his experiences, his values and his dreams, his development of craftsmanship and his endowment of talents. His writing is a part of his mind and his heart. It is a piece of the privacy of his inner being that he has pushed out into the openness of public acceptance or public disapproval or public indifference.

What must a writer have in order to write good books for children? He must have discipline of thought and work habits. He must have values, judgments, balance, and a sense of humor. He must have an involvement with the children of his day, their knowledge, their needs and their desires, their problems and their frustrations. More today than at any other time in our history, a writer does not dare sit in any kind of tower to ponder and to pen. He must go where the children are—into the city streets, the alleyways, the rural roadsides, the parks and playgrounds, the schools and homes. He must see what they see, feel what they feel, and understand the why of their actions and reactions.

I do not mean that all writing should concern itself with

today's activities. Most of it, perhaps, but not all of it. There should be books written about life in other times. A writer should dare to look into the future, he should dare to look into the past. He should dare to wander in a world of fantasy.

In today's world, most of the people are not "sick." Most of their standards are not rotted with greed or hate. We are a nation composed of many kinds of people of different backgrounds, different abilities, and different temperaments. The liquid in any active melting pot will from time to time boil and bubble and froth and foam, but the liquid beneath the effervescence remains clear and sweet and good. For this reason a writer has an obligation to write of a future that is the outgrowth of the past to remind our children that froth and foam exhaust themselves in gaseous escape. This does not change the liquid.

We should not look at our past with shame. We are people who behave like people. If through some of the actions of our past we are able to recognize the wrongs and try to right them, there is hope for us as a nation and as a people. We need not carry the guilt of yesterday's mistakes, only the responsibility to rectify them. Some of our books should remind our children that the people of our past were strong people who lived within the standard structure of their times. We cannot blame the people of hundreds of years ago for not having used today's measuring stick, not if we have learned anything in the centuries between. At any age it is difficult to see the forest for the trees. Only from the distances of space and time are we able to see the shape of things.

What is a book to a writer? It is a record penned with understanding and with hope. It is an imagination. It is a truth.

What is a book from the illustrator's viewpoint? It is a part of his life, his beliefs and his experiences, his values and his dreams, his development of craftsmanship and his endowment of talent. It is an understanding and an interpretation of the writer's meaning. What does an illustrator do for a story? From ideas, he brings forth reality in pictures that must portray the spirit, the setting, the time, the characters, and the action that the writer has described with words in sentences. In addition, through the power and the gift of the illustrator, his pictures can widen and deepen and enrich the story experiences.

What is a book from the viewpoint of the person who buys or selects it for a child reader? First there is content. What a book "says" must be interesting to the child who reads it or listens to it read to him. The story must be vital to him. He must be able to "live it" as the pages turn. It must enrich the world he knows and lead him into a wider, larger unfamiliar world. The experience of having known it must have been an adventure and a delight. It need not have any profound message, but it must have a value and a quality. Every book of fiction has its surface story for all who read to know, but a good book has an inner quality that may have a deep, personal, special meaning for some child, somewhere. It is an unfortunate adult who does not remember certain books of his childhood that he will hold forever dear.

Once a teacher from a school in California wrote me saying that one of their problem children had been a boy who wanted to play the part of Cusi's teacher in *Secret of the Andes*. Those in authority had told him that he could not play the part until he became more like the character. The teacher wrote that they had waited until the end of the year to give the play and the boy had played the part because he had changed his ways. Through the years I have wondered, Did he really change? Was the change lasting? Could the story really have been a small factor in the change? Writers live upon hope.

Another time a boy wrote me that he owned two books, his Bible and one of mine. I have forgotten whether it was *Secret of the Andes* or *Santiago*. Years afterward I was in Little Rock, Arkansas, and looked him up. He was a taxi driver. When I asked him, "Do you still have those two books?" he did not look at me, but he answered, "Yes."

There are other things besides story content. Style can enliven or hamper. Is the writing vivid? Does it have strength? The quality of writing, the expressions used, the descriptive passages, the use of words, and the turn of sentences can be rewarding in many ways.

We discuss maturity and achievement levels. If the child is interested in the story, he is, probably, mature enough to understand it. However, a book that is too difficult for a child to read with ease will neither be enjoyed nor completed. Too-rigid vocabulary control kills a book for all time —not only now, but it kills the desire for future reading. Some writers can limit words and use repetition, and retain both simplicity and beauty, but not all writers have this ability. I never throw away a word merely because it is difficult if it has some purpose to the sentence and to the story. I never use many difficult words, but used sparingly they make good seasoning. A little boy wrote me, "There are too many hard words, but I like them because they sound so pretty."

Book format is another consideration to keep in mind. What about its size? Is it too heavy for little hands to hold? Is it big enough for bigger hands? Are the inner margins of a picture book for the picture-book age wide enough to permit it to lie flat when opened? Will its binding wear well? A book that is loved gets hard use. It does not sit upon a shelf and keep its pages clean and its cover unfrayed. What about type size? Is the type large enough and clear enough and *right* for the one who reads it? I have seen books discarded because the type was small, making it seem difficult to read. But never will too-large type lure a reluctant reader. He considers it "baby stuff" and would be ashamed to be seen reading it. Even the thickness of a book can have significance. For the beginner or slow or reluctant reader these factors have great importance. There must be neither strain nor stress nor fear of impending failure to mar the promise of reading pleasure. A too-thick book seems such an impossible undertaking for the child who is new at reading or who is being coaxed to read.

All my experience has been with readers who have a language handicap and who could become—or remain— nonreaders. There are, of course, some children who seem to live to read. But even with these bookworms care should be taken to help them select the books that are right for them at any given time.

What is a book to the child who reads it? It can become a part of his life, his beliefs, his values, and his dreams. It can be a haven. It can be an adventure. It can be a bridge between two worlds. Why does a child read a book? There are as many reasons as there are children who read and books to be read. A child can read for the pleasure of the sound and the sight and the feel of the words. He can read for information; for instruction or guidance. He can read for escape. He can read to fill an empty span of time.

Children need books and books need children, and we who write, illustrate, and publish them, we who buy and give them must realize that our small world is a reading world and the greatest service we can give our children is to teach them to read, to interpret the meanings, to weigh with judgment, and to use or discard each written sentence according to its value.

EIGHT

Mountain Meadow

"How did you happen to write *Secret of the Andes?*" That question has met me at every turn. One night I sat me down to think it out—how had I come to the writing of that book? Had it been an inspiration of a moment? No. Had it been a long-cherished dream at last fulfilled? No. It had been a very uneventful, natural writing. It had been an easy book to write. It had been a gradual piling up of all that I had learned, and of all that I believed.

My thoughts kept marching back and back until I was a child again in Las Vegas, New Mexico, the town of my birth. What did I remember of that mountain-meadow town? What kind of place was it, this early home of mine? What had it done to me, the child who was born there and who grew up there? Did this small town have anything to do with an Indian herdboy of Peru who came to life in the pages of a book a half century later?

I think it did. I think it had much to do with my writing *Secret of the Andes.*

"Mountain Meadow" is Ann Nolan Clark's Newbery Award acceptance speech, given in 1953 and published in *The Horn Book* (Copyrighted, 1953 by The Horn Book, Incorporated, Boston).

I remember the town of my childhood more vividly, I think, than I know the town it has grown to be. I remember it as a low-walled town of flat-roofed houses—there were fewer than a dozen two-stories then—of dust-filled streets, of the wild-rose-bordered *acequia madre* and rows of giant, twisted cottonwood trees.

I remember Billy Welles, the old stonecutter, and Teddy Roosevelt and his Rough Riders. I remember my mother's velvet riding habit and the fringes on her surrey. I remember the dressed-up dandies driving two-wheeled carts in the narrow streets and the flowing black cape that my grandfather wore.

I remember the horsecars and the horses in the horsecar barn down by the railroad track, and the Street of Tears where little girls were not allowed to walk, and the candle-lighted church at evening where row after row of black-shawled women "told their beads" in whispered Spanish.

I remember Saturday's Bread—I think that is what we called it—a custom of that early day where every household baked great panfuls of bread loaves to give to the poor who came to the door on Saturday.

I remember old Manuela in our kitchen who flip-flapped plate-size tortillas between her hands and baked them on the stove top for my brothers and my little sister and me to eat when our mother was not looking.

I remember Juana because we loved her so. Juana was an old Apache Indian who belonged to the French family across the way. She had been one of five given to this family by their grandfather.

In the early days in New Mexico it had been a custom of

the great feudal families of Spanish Colonial times for a young blood to present his bride-to-be with young Indian girls whom he had captured on a raid. There were a few of these, old women then, still living when I was a child. I think they had never been treated as slaves but as loved members of the household. I know that Juana was a loved and respected matriarch. She was devoted to the three French children with whom we played, and it seemed to my brothers and me that she loved us, too, because she was so good to us.

So many things come crowding back into my memory. Candles set in paper bags half-filled with sand, placed on the roofs of all the houses and lighted for fiestas, fagot bonfires before the house doors at Christmas, and the sad Penitente processions of Holy Week in the hills of Alcalde and Cordova and in the valley towns of the Pecos.

But what has this hodgepodge of memories to do with a boy called Cusi in the Andean highlands? I think it has much to do with my understanding of a boy like Cusi.

It was the days of early Las Vegas that set the pattern for my thinking. It set the pattern for my acceptance of people and folkways and traditions. It set the pattern which the years have deepened.

New Mexico gave to its early children many culture patterns. It gave us the culture pattern of the Indians who lived in our houses and who slept by our fires. When Juana sang to me and washed my face and fed me, she gave me more than acts or words. She gave me an at-homeness with things Indian and primitive.

New Mexico gave us the culture pattern of the Colonial

Spanish who lived on their vast land grants. As children we saw the strip of carpet stretched on the ground from the surrey to the church steps for the Doña to walk upon. We knew that the golden beads and bracelets and bangles that she wore had been mined at the family gold mine and designed for her by the family craftsman. We knew that she had servants to do her will. We also saw her feed those servants, tend them in their illnesses, and care for their well-being. We grew up knowing the responsibility of service to the person who serves you. We accepted this belief.

Even as children we knew about violence. We knew about gun fights. We had them in the streets of our town. We knew about sheep and cattle wars. They were still being fought—at least with words—when I was growing up. We knew about the Flagellantes. We accepted these as other ways of living, not ours, perhaps, but those of our neighbors.

New Mexico gave us the culture of the French trapper, his ways of dress, his manner of speech, his tradition. Mora and Taos were the trapper towns. I went there often with my father. I remember them as exciting and gay and vivid and alive. I do not know why they were, but this is the way I remember them. As children we knew about the Hudson's Bay Company. It might not have been in operation then, but we knew its people living in Mora and Taos, Santa Fé and Las Vegas.

New Mexico gave us the culture pattern of the people "from the states." It was a culture pattern made up of many nationalities, each clinging stubbornly to the European customs and traditions of its forebears. I know our household clung to ours. Our grandfather saw to it. I know that, as well as being a little Indian, a little Spanish, a little French in our ways and our thinking, and "back East" because of Mother and Father, we were above and beyond and completely Irish because Grandfather said so.

All this gave understanding and tolerance and acceptance and appreciation and ease with different peoples who have other ways of thinking and other ways of living.

New Mexico gave that to all her early children, and for me it has made my life way rich and warm and wide.

When I grew up and left Las Vegas for greener pastures, it was natural that I chose my classrooms among the kinds of people I knew best. I have worked with Spanish children from New Mexico to Central and South America, with Indian children from Canada to Peru. I have worked with them because I like them. I write about them because their stories need to be told. All children need understanding, but children of segregated racial groups need even more. All children need someone to make a bridge from their world to the world of the adults who surround them. Indian children need this; they have the child problems of growing up, but also they have racial problems, the problems of conflicting interracial patterns between groups, and the conflicts of changing racial patterns within the group. Any way you look at it, it's rugged to be a child. Often I think more of us did not survive the experience than meets the eye.

I remember my first week with a classroom of six-year-olds in Zuñi. The classroom was full of high, oversize, old-fashioned desks nailed to the floor. That first morning I was late —I had come fifty miles by mail truck. When I entered the room, forty six-year-olds were sitting patiently at the too-big desks, but as I looked at them, they disappeared. Forty six-year-olds went under their desks and there they stayed. They were not naughty or noisy. They were not defiant. They felt frightened and trapped, and sought only for cover. I will never forget my long, long time of waiting while slowly, reluctantly the brave ones came up for air.

I thought of that incident perhaps twenty-five years later in an Indian settlement in the tropic lands of Costa Rica. I was visiting an inland village, so inland there were no roads to it. We flew in by plane and rode to the school on mule-back. We wanted to visit Tito, whom we had heard of—a wonderful, natural teacher. Tito welcomed us and he tried to talk to us, but in the middle of each conversation, it would prove too much for him. When this happened, Tito turned his back and we waited quietly until he felt that he could turn around again.

Adults so take for granted that what they say means the same thing to the listeners as it does to the person who says it. I am reminded again of this same Zuñi school months later, when everyone had come up out of the refuge of an under-the-desk world. I had told this group of six-year-olds the story of Columbus and the three ships that sailed so bravely on the unknown sea. The children decided they would draw a picture of the story. When they brought it to me, I saw a Navajo shepherd and his sheep. "What is this?" I asked them. They told me proudly, "One Colum' and three ships."

This same class once crowded around a new boy who had been sent to school from the pueblo. The children were doubled up with merriment, but the new child in the center of the circle was not amused. When I coaxed them to share the joke, they told me, "This new boy, he say he like it here."

Indians have wonderful mental balance. Generations ago they learned that what cannot be cured must be endured. I do not like morals in stories—at least not if they show. But often I think that groups of children have messages for other groups of children and for adults also. I have taught North American Indian children for twenty years.* I have known these children in all sorts of situations, in Give-away get-togethers of the Dakota Sioux, in tight little complex villages of the Pueblos, in lonely Navajo hogans, and in the cotton-fields of the Papago. Each group and each child has had some message, some story to tell.

At a pueblo school in an Indian village on the Rio Grande in New Mexico, there was a boy, Carlos, overage and over-serious. He believed in the white man's God, in the white man's schoolbooks, and in the teacher; and he hoped worriedly that he could get along with all of them. He was not certain what they meant or what they asked for, but he wanted to get along with them. Every day we had "spelling" and every day was the same story. Carlos studied his lesson diligently, prayed devotedly, and then wrote all the words incorrectly. It never varied. It was always the same. Carlos never gave up hope that someday God and the teacher and the books could come to some kind of compromise and he could meet it.

Many years later I thought of Carlos when some co-workers in Latin America were telling me about a threatened revolu-

* in 1953

tion in Bolivia. The village where these teachers were stationed had been invited to join the revolution, but they said, "It's this way: These North Americans are here and they are such funny people. They do not like revolutions. They might go home if we have one here. But who knows what may happen? Someday, perhaps, they will learn to like revolutions and then we may join you. It does not necessarily follow that what is true today will be true tomorrow."

I could keep on telling stories. One about a Guatemalan boy and his father who walked fifteen miles in a tropic downpour to bring me the live family rooster so I could take it with me and have the man on the plane cook it for me when I was hungry. About my own small boy on his first communal Indian rabbit drive, who, when I asked him why he said he had killed half a rabbit, said, "It lay down and was dead for a little while and then it got up and ran off." About Pat, my small grandson, who said to me, "Look, Grandmother, even the flowers are glad to see us. Look how they are bowing to us."

These are the reasons I write about children. If the children like what I write, that's a gift to me from my grandfather's fairies in Ireland.

The children I write about are part of all the children I have known. They are part of their laughter and their dreams, their hurts and their brave, big hopes. They are the children who have walked with me and talked with me and have been my friends.

I knew Cusi in *Secret of the Andes* under many other names and in many other places. I also knew him in the market place in Cuzco.

To answer other questions that have been asked me, I know Peru. I have lived there. I know its roads and its mountain trails, its misted peaks and its age-old ruins. I knew Cusi. I knew him in Peru. I knew him in Ecuador. All my life I have been getting ready to understand him. *Secret of the Andes* is part fact, part imagination, part legend— all so mixed up together that for me it happened.

If I could have a wish come true for the people who follow me in receiving the Newbery Medal, it is that they do not receive this great honor too soon in their writing career, or too early in their years of living. I wish this because I believe to get its richest, headiest flavor the trail to it must have been long and rough and slow in climbing to make the thirst for its nectar deep and good.

NINE

Full Sunlight

When I received the letter saying that the Regina Medal was to be mine, given to me because of service, I could not believe it. The Regina Medal is such a tremendous honor and it came so quietly. With other awards there is always hope that perhaps someday, someday in the faraway future, one might be good enough to be so honored, but the Regina Medal was space-miles beyond and above any daydream of mine.

Inner questionings began clamoring for answers. Did I deserve this honor? Why had it happened to me? What had enabled me to reach a place where this medal could be mine?

There were certain facts I knew. I knew them with clarity and honesty. My receiving this award could not be for what I am. I fall far short of any measure of greatness. It could not be for knowledge. I have little knowledge and smaller wisdom. It could not be for writing gift. There are those

"Full Sunlight," in slightly different form, was Ann Nolan Clark's Regina Medal acceptance speech, given in 1963.

with greater story sense. There are those with greater force and power in writing skills.

What then did I have that brought me this honor?

Answers came to mind and were discarded for newer ones. There was one that kept returning. Like a small persistent voice it kept worrying at the edges of my thoughts. It kept on and on repeating, "If it is not for what you are or know or can do, it must be for something that you believe. . . ." Something that you believe?

What I believe? What do I believe? The teachings of my faith, of course. But I was born in my faith. My faith is my heritage. I have not suffered in its growth within me, nor— not yet—in its defense.

I asked myself, "What is this belief that has not been given to me, nor laid down before me, but I, myself, have developed? Was it born because of something I have seen or people I have met in my journeying through life?"

Gradually the answer came. It must be because of my belief that people need people, that an acceptance of people by people is important and necessary and vital.

I believe that acceptance of people by people is not built with words nor treaties nor resolutions for coexistence.

It is built upon tolerance—tolerance for other people's values. It is built upon respect—respect for the traditions and customs of other nationalities, races, and culture. It is built with sharing—sharing of experiences of the tangibles and intangibles of everyday living among the peoples of the world.

Why do I have this belief? When did it become a part of

me? Where did I find it? How has it been nourished? Answers to these questions, I thought, would perhaps explain to me why I had received an award for service.

I turned my thoughts backward—backward as far as I could remember and picked my memories at random—not for their importance, not in absolute sequence, but just as they occurred to me. These memories I give to you. I give them to you in pieces, small fragments, falling into place, making a pattern, a pattern that has directed me and shaped the output of my heart and mind.

The first memories I have are of the New Mexico town where I was born and of the people of the town. Las Vegas was a frontier settlement surrounded by meadows and mesas and mountains. It was a town of dusty streets and wooden sidewalks. The old houses were of adobe with bright-blue doors opening onto sun-filled portals and patios. The newer houses were of hand-cut stone with second stories and porches with railings. The very new houses, not as many as half a dozen probably, were of frame with gingerbread scrollwork and wide verandas. As I remember, we did not entirely approve of those very new houses, or was it of the people who lived in them? To us they were the newcomers, as we were, I suppose, to the Indians and the Spanish.

Our house was of stone, hand-cut by the town's stonemason, a remittance man. "Kicked out of England," my grandfather said, "as fine a man as ever was." There was pride in my Irish grandfather's voice for a man so bad that England would not keep him.

My mother's best friend was the French woman who lived in a stone house across the way.

My father's special cronies were Don José, a Spanish grandee, and Uncle Charlie, a Jewish merchant who was called Uncle by all the children of the town. "Don José is of the Old School," said Grandfather Nolan with hearty approval and Uncle Charlie, he told us, was a great one for turning a penny. This last was said with a smidgen of envy.

My special hero of that day was Mr. Thomas Delaney, a bald-headed, peg-legged gentleman straight from the heart of Killarney. He ran what was called "The Short-Order Restaurant." My mother forbade me to taste a mouthful of the food he served, but it was delicious. I could have told her.

Irish, English, French, Spanish, Indian, German perhaps, although at the moment I cannot remember. "Salt of the earth," my grandfather described them. "Although not Irish, mind you," he told us, "in their own way good people, all of them."

They were our neighbors, our friends, part of our lives, a handful of families in a frontier town. Each family fiercely proclaiming its own nationality and cheerfully following all the national customs and traditions of the other families as well as its own.

On Guadalupe Day everyone lighted *farolitas* of piñon firewood in front of his house, one for each member of the family. It was town pride to know that Las Vegas did its share to light the way of Our Lady of Guadalupe from the City of Old Mexico to Taos Pueblo, New Mexico.

When the earth was parched in summer we went to the Indian pueblos to watch the age-old ceremonial dances for rain. We watched the Indians, painted and bedecked almost beyond our recognition, circle and swirl and stoop and stamp to the drumbeats of their chorus. We felt the drumbeat in the air around us. We felt its throb swell upward from the heart of the earth and we rejoiced with the Indians that their dancing had made the rain to fall.

On the French Bastille Day there was always a great to-do with parties at our house, your house, and everyone's house and a grand dance in the evening with candles instead of the lamplight of an ordinary evening.

There were the Jewish religious occasions that we shared, solemn and serious, our best manners showing.

On Saint Patrick's Day everyone was Irish. My grandfather made his fiddle cry and sing and my mother jigged when my father coaxed her.

French, Spanish, English, Indian, Irish! Those were the days when Dublin town and Taos and Paris and all of Spain and "County Cook" (my grandfather's name for Chicago) were just beyond the nearest hill.

We did not know such words as "acceptance" and "tolerance." We did not need to know them.

Then came the days of the war that made the world safe for democracy. Remember? With it came the heady thrill of patriotism and an awareness of the United States as our nation. We knew, of course, that the United States had always been close by, but we had been too busy being part of our town to be aware that we were also part of our nation. Now we welcomed it. We took the whole of it into our town and into our hearts. And of course, as was bound to happen, it took us, too.

The gates of my life at this time opened, not very wide, but wide enough for me to slip through. The years that followed the First World War were very gay, although I cannot remember now what made them so. My memories tell me only that they were made up of happenings and not of people.

Some time during this period I learned how to teach. Mabel Parsons was the first to teach me. A funny idea this New Yorker had, that teachers should know the home life of the children they taught. I was willing to learn. My training had always been to be one with the people around me. It was at this time I came to know the warm, generous, wonderful people of a wild and violent mining town, the Slav and Italian coal miners. They shared everything they had with us, their rich, spicy foods, their babies to godmother, their fights and feuds, their homemade wine. They brought a new richness into my life. What I gave to them I do not know.

After a time my life way forked and I went to teach Indians in Indian schools. I brought the knowledge I had learned with me, how to merge my life with theirs so I could know what to teach them to treasure; what to suggest that they put behind them; what to show them to look for in their new tomorrows.

Then came my years of discipline. In among them was World War II. When my son, a pilot, flew into the "wild blue yonder," I saw him go with pride in his courage.

During this time I went with a team from the Indian bureau to help set up a school program at a Japanese-American relocation camp. I did not want to go there. But Mr. Beatty, my "boss" and my friend, told me I had to go. "If anything happens to Tom," he said, "I want you to know that

Japanese are people." I went. Years afterward one of the Japanese teachers took her vacation time to come to Chicago where I was working, to tell me, "I am sorry my people did this to you."

These were my years of discipline. At their ending my life gate had opened wide—and I went forth upon the unfamiliar trails that lay open before me to the *altos planos* and jungle trails and sandy coastlands of Central and South America.

A new depth of understanding came to me. I was not only Irish, a New Mexican, a citizen of the United States; I now became a North American who must recognize responsibility, feel compassion, extend mercy, offer help to those who needed it.

Memories come swifter here, come crowding, come demanding each one its place. They become individual and personal and yet each one helps to prove that people need people and that acceptance of people by people can be a reality rather than a hope.

The time came in Costa Rica when a blood transfusion was my slender bridge between life and death. In that small country then, blood banks were unknown, unheard of. The giving of blood by one person to another was terrible and frightening, a sharing with another one's own precious life-spark that God Himself had given. I was a newcomer, a foreigner, a stranger and yet the hospital corridor was filled with volunteers. The one chosen to give me his blood was the leading Communist of the country. They said he insisted that he had too much blood and he demanded that he be allowed to share it with the little teacher who needed it. I saw him once and then he went his way, but he left with me the strength to live again.

In one school in Costa Rica, a group of aristocratic urban teachers swept my classroom—not because they believed in manual work, they told me in careful, formal Spanish. It was beneath their class. "But you," they told me, "being a North American, have peculiar values concerning work and so we are willing to do this for you."

I could go on and on telling of people of our country and of other countries, people of town and settlement, pueblo and encampment, in the cool, dark rain forests, on the wind-swept *altos planos,* in the muggy coastal swamps, on the wide sand stretches; people of the Americas who accept strangers, who tolerate strange values, who respect strange customs and who share with others all that they have. They are every-where. They need only to be found and to be told about. I think especially do they need to be written about in our books for children. Children need to know that tolerance and respect, sharing and giving are a natural way of life for many, many people.

So thus I look backward, seeing fragments of my life's journey fitted together in a pattern of places and happenings and people—mostly of people. I look ahead and the way is misted. I cannot see what lies before me. But today I stand in full sunlight and I am mindful as to how I have reached this place. It is because of my belief in people, and people, themselves, have given me this belief. Therefore, for the people I have met on the trail, for those who have passed me, for the many who have traveled with me a short or a longer way, and for the few who have walked beside me the weary and the merry mile, for all these people and in their names I accept with humility and gratitude the Regina Medal for the Year of Our Lord 1963.

TEN

Talisman

Mountain peaks loomed black, forbidding, against a background of gray night. Little lost winds cried lonesomely, cried forsakenly, as they wandered on the mountain slopes. Stars hung low, brooding, over the mountains and the sleeping valley. The air of Andean Ecuador was thin and piercingly cold.

Slowly the mountain peaks changed from black to blue; slowly the night sky lightened, and the peaks were etched clearly against the dawn. Slowly the mountain slopes awakened. There was no sound, but there was movement, a life pulse in the somberness of sleep.

Small fire flames lighted the doorways of the thatch-roofed houses that were perched on ridges, tilted against rocks, and nestled in the folds of the slopes. Small figures moved around each tiny fire flame, moved about in each house-door garden and through each patchwork field outlined by its cactus fences.

Slowly the fire flames died, and smoke ribbons curled up

"Talisman" was printed by The Viking Press as a place favor for the 1963 Regina Medal presentation dinner.

into the early morning. Slowly the night mist rose up from the valley to shroud the foot of the mountains until only the tips of the peaks could be seen crowned in the bright glory of the new day.

Suddenly every hut in its patch of field poured out a stream of people—men, women, children wrapped in ponchos and blankets against the highland cold. They poured from their houses of thatch and wattle. They came from their gardens and fields. They came to shoulder their heavy burden packs and to begin their journey to the market town far below on the floor of the valley.

They were Andean Indians of Ecuador—small, sturdy, highland people. They came, an unending line, always in single file, always with a swaying, running movement, swiftly, silently along the narrow, deeply rutted trailways, zigzagging down, steeply down, all the mountain slopes.

Soon all the trailways were filled with running people, barefoot, blanket-wrapped, their backs bent low under the great burdens they carried. The peopled lines grew and merged and swelled as the trail ways emptied into the roadways. Thick yellow dust clouds seemed to flow above the line of movement. Now the patter of uncountable running feet, the swish of ponchos and blankets hummed into the silence. The thin bleatings of frightened goats, herded by determined boy herders, and the squealings of protesting pigs being dragged along on gay-colored hand-woven leashes cut through the dust clouds. But there was no talk or laughter or song. Mostly, the world of the highland Andes is a silent world.

This was market day. All the roadways led to the plaza of

the market town and soon it was filled with milling Indians. Enclosing the town plaza were the white-plaster-walled and red-tile-roofed houses of the mestizos, people of Indian and Spanish blood. The blue house doors were closed at this early hour. Not until later would the black-shawled mestizo women venture forth, bringing their servants to carry the vegetables and woolens, pottery and poultry that each would buy from a favorite vendor.

At this hour of sunrise the market belonged to the Indians. They came from the other side of the mountains and from across the lake and up from the jungle trails, as well as from the mountain slopes that rimmed the valley. They came then as they had come since prehistoric times, to barter or sell their garden stuff and their handwork, to trade for or to buy what they needed and wanted, and to rest from daily toil.

The brilliant peaks, the sparkling air, the milling Indians, and the riot of colors were exhilarating and at the same time confusing and exhausting. There were colors, moving colors that blended softly and contrasted sharply, a sea of colors that moved with the moving people.

The market pattern was as ancient and as rigid and un-changing as the mountains that rimmed the market town. Each community had its special wares, had its own place fanning out from the heart of the plaza. The ponchos and shawls, cottons and woolens, made a splash of vivid, bold rainbow colors—red, blue, and purple, violet and turquoise, rose, green, and gold. There were tapestry belts and blouses embroidered in crimson yarn, head scarves and shawls hung on lines like bright butterflies swaying in the icy wind.

There was pattern and design in the display of wares, but the visitor remembers only a wild confusion of things—mats and leather goods, pottery and wooden chests, bundles of raw wool, pinches of dyes, herbs and medicines, charms and spices, scissors and old iron keys, trinkets and treasures, soap and soup, salt and tallow.

The night mist had melted away, and the sun shone bright and clear. My friend and I had come mostly to see the people. We had wanted to watch them pour down the steep sides of the mountains and flow from bank to bank along the roadways. We had wanted to watch them come into the plaza, each to his age-old place. We wanted to be one with them as each silently bowed his head in prayer, blessing his wares and the place where he would sell them. We wanted to see if it was really true that the proceeds from each first sale would be set aside as a thank offering to church or charity. These small people, so very poor, scratching with their hands their life food from the steep, rocky slopes of the mountains, were rich in gratitude.

We had not come to buy. We had come to mingle with the people and to share with them their market day.

At last we came to that part of the market where trinkets were sold—brass rings with settings of colored glass, strings of coral and glass beads, silver and copper earrings.

My friend was the first to see a treasure among the trinkets lying on a piece of cloth. She saw it and bought it, and showed it to me. I loved it at once; it was something I had to have. So she gave it to me—a thin silver cross. At least we *thought* it was silver. It was so tarnished, so blackened and dirty, that we were not certain until a long time afterward, when I had washed it and polished it and washed and polished it again and again. Then we could see the curious inscription on it. But at first it was only a thin tarnished cross of a peculiar shape.

I wore it on a string of Zuñi silver beads almost all the time. At parties in Central and South America it was called "the conversation cross" because it was always good for a lively discusion. Every Latin who saw it was interested in it, and each had his own name for it and his own explanation of its inscription.

The cross is such an ancient symbol, worn and used ages before the birth of Christ. It is of many shapes and designs and has many meanings. After it became the symbol of Christianity, it still was formed differently by the different peoples who used it, shaped by the fancy of the man or the company of men who took it as their emblem.

Ten years after I had found mine at the sunrise market in a highland village of Ecuador I happened to be in Panama. A friend and I walked down the little street of shops where all the marketable treasures of the world were on display for buying.

Again we had come to look and to see and to be part of the milling people. Idly we stopped at the open door of a silver shop. The proprietor, as is usual in those places, stood at the door to singsong his wares and ask the passersby to come in to make purchases. But I, instead of being asked to buy, was asked to sell the cross I was wearing. "It is not for sale," I told the man.

"Don't you know what you have?" he asked me. "That cross is the Cross of Lorraine. It is a cross of the Crusaders."

A cross of the Crusaders? The Cross of Lorraine? Perhaps it is. It has the same two "thwarts" that distinguish the cross that Godfrey is believed to have carried with him on the First Crusade—Godfrey, the tall, blue-eyed, golden-haired Frank, hero of the battle in which Jerusalem was taken from the infidels! He was chosen to be first king of Jerusalem, but he refused, saying that he could not wear a crown of gold where his Lord had worn a crown of thorns.

As a boy of seventeen he had defended his mother's castle; yet later, when he had inherited the castle, he sold it, as well as his title of Duke of Lorraine, to raise funds to finance the First Crusade. It would seem logical that he would take to the Holy Land the cross of his dear homeland and of the castle that he had loved and defended and sacrificed.

But if my cross is a cross of the Crusaders, how did it get to the highlands of Ecuador? Did an early conquistador bring it with him as a treasured inheritance from a Crusader-ancestor? Had he given it away? Had he lost it? Had he bartered it for bread?

Perhaps it had been brought by early Jesuits when they came into the wild New World, bringing the cross and the faith to the Indian people.

But that was long ago. Where has the little cross been these centuries? Has it had a special meaning to those who have owned it? Why was it put for sale that one day I went to market? Why did I have to own it?

Could it be destiny? The destiny for those who own it to take the cross and carry on their own crusade?